"The simple truth is this: I needed this book right now! There are truths in this volume—pastoral insights and healing counsels—that speak to me in very personal and tender ways. Occasionally, Murray's point is so clear—far too clear—that it feels as though I have gotten a slap in the face. But always—always—the point has been to drive me to Christ and to drive me to the embrace of the gospel. This is medicine for the soul in the best possible sense, and I am grateful to the author for writing it. It really does feel as though he wrote it for me."

Derek W. H. Thomas, Senior Minister, First Presbyterian Church, Columbia, South Carolina; Robert Strong Professor of Systematic and Pastoral Theology, Reformed Theological Seminary–Atlanta

"This is so timely. After you read it, you will sleep better, for starters. Then you will be taken to the meeting place of essential theology and the details of all things related to our stressed lives, where David offers wisdom on every page. The book is perfect for men's groups."

Ed Welch, counselor; faculty member, the Christian Counseling and Educational Foundation

"For far too long, whether consciously or subconsciously, we Christians have bought into the platonic lie that the spirit matters, but the body does not. As a result, we have neglected, and perhaps even abused, our bodies. It's no wonder we struggle with food, sleep, and health—both physical and mental. In *Reset*, David Murray returns us to a biblical anthropology, providing us with a biblical and theological framework by which we may reorder our lives as whole persons—body and spirit—for God's glory, our well-being, and the service of others."

Juan R. Sanchez, Senior Pastor, High Pointe Baptist Church, Austin, Texas; author, *1 Peter for You* and *Gracia Sobre Gracia*

"From a vast reservoir of personal experience, authenticating social research, and timeless theological wisdom, David Murray shines illuminating light on the dark perils of pastoral burnout. He also offers practical guidance for how the easy yoke of apprenticeship with Jesus makes possible the grace-paced life that leads to personal and vocational wholeness. I highly recommend this needed approach."

Tom Nelson, author, *Work Matters;* Senior Pastor, Christ Community Church, Overland Park, Kansas; President, Made to Flourish

"Men, this wise book is like a personal coach for your daily life. The one who writes it understands what it is to be a man with a man's cares and a man's dreams. He cares deeply about the masculine body and soul that God has given you. You were made with large purpose. David Murray wants to help you learn how to practically take stock of your life, recover your purpose, and live it!"

Zack Eswine, Lead Pastor, Riverside Church, Webster Groves, Missouri; author, *The Imperfect Pastor*

ReSET

Living a Grace-Paced Life
in a Burnout Culture

David Murray

CROSSWAY®

WHEATON, ILLINOIS

Published in association with the literary agency of Legacy, LLC, 501 N. Orlando Avenue, Suite #313–348, Winter Park, FL 32789.

First printing 2017

Printed in the United States of America

Some of the material in this book has appeared in different form on various blogs, including www.headhearthand.org and www.christwardcollective.org. Used with permission.

Unless otherwise indicated, all Scripture quotations are from *The New King James Version*. Copyright © 1982, Thomas Nelson, Inc. Used by permission.

Scripture references marked NIV are taken from The Holy Bible, New International Version®, NIV®. Copyright © 1973, 1978, 1984, 2011 by Biblica, Inc.™ Used by permission. All rights reserved worldwide.

All emphases in Scripture quotations have been added by the author.

Trade paperback ISBN: 978-1-4335-5518-3
ePub ISBN: 978-1-4335-5521-3
PDF ISBN: 978-1-4335-5519-0
Mobipocket ISBN: 978-1-4335-5520-6

Library of Congress Cataloging-in-Publication Data

Names: Murray, David P., author.
Title: Reset : living a grace-paced life in a burnout culture / David Murray.
Description: Wheaton : Crossway, 2017. | Includes bibliographical references and index.
Identifiers: LCCN 2016016684 (print) | LCCN 2016037420 (ebook) | ISBN 9781433555183 (tp) | ISBN 9781433555190 (pdf) | ISBN 9781433555206 (mobi) | ISBN 9781433555213 (epub)
Subjects: LCSH: Christian men—Religious life. | Burn out (Psychology)—Religious aspects—Christianity.
Classification: LCC BV4528.2 .M865 2017 (print) | LCC BV4528.2 (ebook) | DDC 248.8/42—dc23
LC record available at https://lccn.loc.gov/2016016684

Crossway is a publishing ministry of Good News Publishers.

LB   25   24   23   22   21   20   19   18   17
14   13   12   11   10   9   8   7   6   5   4   3   2   1

To the pastors, elders, and deacons of
Grand Rapids Free Reformed Church.

You have taught me, by word and example,
what it means to be a man of God.

Contents

Introduction... 9

Repair Bay 1: Reality Check 19

Repair Bay 2: Review...37

Repair Bay 3: Rest...53

Repair Bay 4: Re-Create......................................71

Repair Bay 5: Relax 87

Repair Bay 6: Rethink....................................... 105

Repair Bay 7: Reduce.. 123

Repair Bay 8: Refuel.. 141

Repair Bay 9: Relate.. 157

Repair Bay 10: Resurrection 175

Acknowledgments 193

General Index... 195

Scripture Index... 205

Introduction

It was one of the most humiliating moments of my life. I'd just come through a successful winter cross-country season in high school, and spring track was getting under way. Our track coach started us off with a series of 800-meter races to split the middle- and long-distance runners into first and second teams. I didn't train beforehand because I was used to far longer races in far worse conditions.

I knew I had to run a bit faster over the shorter distance, so I took off at the sound of the gun. By the time I was halfway round the first lap, I was a good fifty meters ahead of everyone else. "This is too easy," I thought. I didn't have my usual cross-country signposts to help me gauge my speed, but over such a short race in such beautiful spring weather, what could possibly go wrong?

By the end of the first lap, my lungs were beginning to burst and my fifty-meter lead had become twenty-five. Soon I was overtaken by one runner after another, until one of the poorest runners in my class padded past me with a snicker. At the 600-meter mark, I decided to get "injured" and collapsed in a heap at the side of the track.

I learned the hard way that pacing a race is one of the

most important skills for track athletes to learn. Go too slow and we fail by never winning or fulfilling our potential. Go too fast and we fail by injuring ourselves or running out of energy before the finish line. Finding that perfect pace, that sweet spot between too slow and too fast, is vital for success and longevity as an athlete—and as a Christian.

Speed Up and Slow Down

In recent years, a number of Christian leaders have rightly called lethargic and half-hearted Christians to quicken their pace, to dedicate more of their time, talents, money, and efforts to serving the Lord in the local church and in evangelistic outreach at home and abroad. I welcome this "radical," "don't waste your life" message to up the pace, and I rejoice in its positive impact on thousands of Christians, especially among the younger generations.

There are others, however, many of them faithful and zealous Christians, especially those aged thirty-five-plus, who need to hear a different message: "Slow your pace or you'll never finish the race." As Brady Boyd warned in *Addicted to Busy*, "Ultimately, every problem I see in every person I know is a problem of moving too fast for too long in too many aspects of life."[1] I'm not proposing that we put our feet up and opt out of life and Christian service. No, I'm talking about carefully adjusting to life changes as we age, as responsibilities mount, as families grow, as problems multiply, as energy levels diminish, and as health complications arise. That's what successful pace runners do. They are sensitive to significant changes in themselves and in race conditions, and they recalibrate their

---

1. Brady Boyd, *Addicted to Busy: Recovery for the Rushed Soul* (Colorado Springs: Cook, 2014), 44.

pace to avoid injury or exhaustion, ensuring a happy and successful finish.

I've discovered that such pacing skills are in short supply among Christian men, with the result that too many—especially those most committed to serving Christ in their families, in the workplace, and in the local church—are crashing or fading fast before their race is over. It's not just a "Christian" problem though; it's also a culture problem. Some 225 million workdays are lost every year in the United States due to stress; that's nearly a million people not working every workday.[2] The data on pastors is especially worrying, with high levels of stress, depression, and burnout leading to broken bodies, broken minds, broken hearts, broken marriages, and broken churches. (Burnout is responsible for 20 percent of all pastoral resignations.[3]) That's hardly surprising, since surveys reveal that pastors relegate physical exercise, nutrition, and sleep to a much lower priority than the average worker.[4] I've been there and done that—and suffered the consequences. But through painful personal experience, and also through counseling many others since, I've learned that God has graciously provided a number of ways for us to reset our broken and burned-out lives, and to help us live grace-paced lives in a burnout culture.

Although no two burnouts are the same, as I've counseled increasing numbers of Christians through burnout, I've

2. Richard Swenson, *Margin: Restoring Emotional, Physical, Financial, and Time Reserves to Overloaded Lives* (Colorado Springs: NavPress, 2004), 43–44.

3. Lisa Cannon-Green, "Why 734 Pastors Quit (and How Their Churches Could Have Kept Them)," *Christianity Today*, January 12, 2016, http://www.christianitytoday.com/gleanings/2016/january/why-734-pastors-quit-how-churches-could-have-kept-them.html.

4. Gary Harbaugh, *Pastor as Person: Maintaining Personal Integrity in the Choices and Challenges of Ministry* (Minneapolis: Augsburg Fortress, 1984), 47.

noticed that most of them have one thing in common—there are deficits of grace. It's not that these Christians don't believe in grace. Not at all; all of them are well grounded in "the doctrines of grace," and many of them are pastors who preach grace powerfully every week. The "five solas" and the "five points" are their theological meat and drink. Yet there are disconnects between theological grace and their daily lives, resulting in five deficits of grace.

Five Deficits of Grace

First, the *motivating* power of grace is missing. To illustrate, take a look at five people printing Bibles on the same assembly line. Mr. Dollar is asking, "How can I make more money?" Mr. Ambitious is asking, "How can I get a promotion?" Mr. Pleaser is asking, "How can I make my boss happy?" Mr. Selfish is asking, "How can I get personal satisfaction in my job?" They all look and feel miserable. Then we bump into Mr. Grace, who's asking, "In view of God's amazing grace to me in Christ, how can I serve God and others here?"

From the outside, it looks as if all five are doing the same work, but inside, they look completely different. The first four are striving, stressed, anxious, fearful, and exhausted. But Mr. Grace is so energized by his gratitude for grace that his job satisfies and stimulates him rather than draining him. Where grace is not fueling a person from the inside out, he burns from the inside out.

Also absent is the *moderating* power of grace. Alongside Mr. Grace, Mr. Perfectionist takes pride in flawless performance. If he ever makes a mistake in his work, he berates and flagellates himself. He carries this legalistic perfectionism into his relationships with God and others, resulting in constant disappointment in himself, in others, and even in God.

Mr. Grace's work is just as high quality as Mr. Perfectionist, but grace has moderated his expectations. At the foot of the cross, he has learned that he's not perfect and never will be. He accepts that both his work and his relationships are flawed. But instead of tormenting himself with these imperfections, he calmly takes them to the perfect God, knowing that in his grace, this God forgives every shortcoming and lovingly accepts him as perfect in Christ. He doesn't need to serve, sacrifice, or suffer his way to human or divine approval because Christ has already served, sacrificed, and suffered for him.

Without motivating grace, we just rest in Christ. Without moderating grace, we just run and run—until we run out. We need the first grace to fire us up when we're dangerously cold; we need the second to cool us down when we're dangerously hot. The first gets us out of bed; the second gets us to bed on time. The first recognizes Christ's fair demands upon us; the second receives Christ's full provision for us. The first says, "Present your body a living sacrifice"; the second says, "Your body is a temple of the Holy Spirit." The first overcomes the resistance of our "flesh"; the second respects the limitations of our humanity. The first speeds us up; the second slows us down. The first says, "My son, give me your hands"; the second says, "My son, give me your heart."

The *multiplying* power of grace is also rare in burned-out lives. Back on the assembly line, some of the Christian workers are driven by production targets. If they fall short of their daily quotas of Bibles, they go home totally depressed because "Every Bible we fail to print and package is a soul unreached." As everything depends on their sweat and muscle, they work tons of overtime and hardly have any time for personal prayer.

Mr. Grace, however, works normal hours, and yet he has time and peace to pray for God's blessing on each Bible that passes through his hands. He works hard, but he depends on God's grace to multiply his work. He realizes that while one plants and another waters, God gives the increase. He goes home happy each evening, knowing that he has done what he could, and, as he leaves the factory at 5 p.m., he prays that God will multiply his work far more than his muscles or hours could.

The *releasing* power of grace has often been lacking when a person burns out. Mr. Controller, for example, thinks everything depends on him. He gets involved in every step of the production process, constantly annoying other workers with his micromanagement. He's infuriated by any breakdown in production, yelling at people and even the machines when they mess up. He says he believes in "sovereign grace," but he's the sovereign and grace is limited to personal salvation.

In contrast, Mr. Grace realizes God is sovereign even in the nuts and bolts of life, and releases control of everything into his hands. He works carefully, but humbly submits to setbacks and problems, accepting them as tests of his trust in God's control. In the midst of challenges and setbacks, he can often be heard whispering to himself, "Release, release, release."

Another void in many breakdowns is the *receiving* power of grace. Unlike Mr. Grace, most of his bosses and fellow workers refuse to accept many of God's best gifts. They won't receive the grace of a weekly Sabbath, the grace of sufficient sleep, the grace of physical exercise, the grace of family and friends, or the grace of Christian fellowship. These are all gifts that our loving heavenly Father has provided to refresh and renew his creatures. Yet instead of humbly receiving them, most refuse and reject them, thinking that such graces are for the weak. Yes, it is more blessed to give than to receive. But if we don't do any receiving, our giving soon dries up.

As long as these five grace deficits exist in the lives of Christians, the wrecker's yard is going to keep filling with broken and burned-out believers. But by connecting God's grace more and more to our daily lives—by growing in these five graces—we can learn how to live grace-paced lives in a burnout culture. That's what this book will train you to live out.

Middle-Aged Only?

But this isn't a book just for middle-aged men. Every victim of burnout will tell you that unhealthy patterns of living and working that they learned in their youth caused their downfall later in life. And if any group is in danger today, it's the millennial generation (aged 18–33), whose stress levels are higher than the national average, according to a report by the American Psychological Association. Thirty-nine percent of millennials say their stress has increased in the past year, and 52 percent say stress about work, money, and relationships has kept them awake at night in the past month, with one in five clinically depressed or stressed out and needing medication.[5] As prevention is always better than cure, I hope this book will also help younger men learn how to renew their bodies and souls so that they too start living grace-paced lives instead of joining the statistics.

---

5. Sharon Jayson, "The State of Stress in America," *USA Today*, February 7, 2013, http://www.usatoday.com/story/news/nation/2013/02/06/stress-psychology-millennials-depression/1878295/.

Men Only?

Why write for men only? Don't women also overrun, burn out, get depressed, and so on? Yes, of course they do; but as they often do it in different ways than men, and for different reasons, some of the solutions are different too. That's why my wife, Shona, is joining me to cowrite a sequel to this book, a *Reset for Women,* if you will. As my wife for twenty-five years, a mother of five children (ranging from two to twenty), a family doctor for fifteen years, a past sufferer with depression, and a counselor to many women over many years, Shona will bring a unique female perspective to the problems that women face in this area and to the solutions that can help Christian women live grace-paced lives in a burnout culture.

So, should women put this book down and wait for the female version? No! If you want to understand your husband better and help him live a grace-paced life, keep reading and jog alongside him as you work out together what track God is calling him to run and what speed will get him to the finish line.

Pastors Only?

When Justin Taylor of Crossway originally approached me to write this book, he had in mind a book especially for pastors and other church leaders. I understood and shared Justin's concern for the unique challenges that Christian ministry leaders face in this area. However, among all the emails, phone calls, and office visits I had received from burned-out and stressed-out pastors over the years, I had also gotten many from Christian men in nonministry callings who were struggling with similar challenges and who responded well to similar counsel. That's why we decided the book should be addressed to Christian men in general, but with a regular focus upon Christian ministry leaders in particular. We believe that this is the best way to help the greatest number of Christian men and pastors discover how to reset their lives and enjoy the healthy balance of grace motivation and grace moderation exemplified by the apostle:

> Therefore we also, since we are surrounded by so great a cloud of witnesses, let us lay aside every weight, and the sin which so easily ensnares us, and let us run with endurance the race that is set before us, looking unto Jesus, the author and finisher of our faith, who for the joy that was set before Him endured the cross, despising the shame, and has sat down at the right hand of the throne of God. (Heb. 12:1–2)

Reality Check

↻

"You have multiple blood clots in both lungs."

Just a few hours earlier, I had been reading and relaxing in a chair at home when I felt a sudden tightness in my neck area, a building pressure that then spread down my chest and arms. It was painful, but not unbearable. I was breathless, hot, and disoriented.

Although the symptoms lasted only about ten minutes, my wife, Shona (an experienced family physician), was adamant that further investigation was needed. But when we arrived at the local emergency room, I felt fairly normal again, so I spent ten minutes trying to persuade her that we should just go home rather than waste a few hours and hundreds of dollars on a pointless ER visit. Thankfully, Shona prevailed and I agreed to go in, my parting comment being, "I'm doing this for you, not me!" (Poor woman!)

Although the results of the heart tests were normal and the doctor felt 95 percent certain that all was fine, he said that it was best to get my blood enzymes checked at the downtown hospital just to be certain that there had been no heart attack. As I dithered, Shona decided, "Yes, we're going."

At the hospital, I happened to mention to the doctor that I had had a pain in my calf muscle since Sunday morning, which I breezily dismissed as "probably a muscle strain from tae kwon do." He paused, turned back toward me, and narrowed his eyes: "Have you traveled recently?" I said that I had driven to Canada on Friday and arrived back in Grand Rapids on Monday morning.

The doctor looked concerned and decided to screen my blood, just to rule out a deep vein thrombosis (DVT) in my leg. An hour later (just after midnight), the results came back with a very high positive. For the first time, alarm bells began to ring in my mind.

Next, I was sent off for a CAT scan. Thirty minutes later, I heard the life-changing (and possibly life-ending) words, "I'm afraid you have multiple blood clots in both lungs [pulmonary emboli], probably having spun off from a clot in your leg." I was told to lie flat on the bed and be as still as possible lest more clots break off from my leg and block my lungs. I was given a large dose of heparin and an intravenous drip of the same to stabilize the clots and start thinning my blood.

The next thirty-six hours were deeply solemnizing. All the blood clot anecdotes I'd heard over the years decided to flood my mind, probably partly provoked by the doctor's parting words: "Don't move from the bed; you have a life-threatening condition." A sleepless blur of tests, tests, and more tests followed throughout the day, with fluctuating results: raising my hopes, then disappointing and worrying me.

Good to Be Afflicted?

In one of the rare moments of privacy I managed to grab in the maelstrom of that first night in the hospital, I picked up a daily devotional book beside my bed and turned to that day's date to find meditations on the following verses:

> I called on the LORD in distress; the LORD answered me and set me in a broad place. (Ps. 118:5)

> It is good for me that I have been afflicted, that I may learn Your statutes. (Ps. 119:71)

These two themes—thankfulness to God for graciously delivering me and a desire to learn from this trauma—stayed with me for the next few days. The primary lesson was painfully clear: "God's been hunting me down."

That was my immediate and instinctive understanding of why the Lord had sent these blood clots into my leg and lungs. Three weeks and two complications later, I was more convinced than ever that God had been tracking me for many months, with loving arrow after loving arrow, until at last he'd brought me down to the dust.

Up until a year before, I'd lived a more or less healthy and vigorous life. At 6 feet 3 inches and 186 pounds, I was on the light side of average. Work and ministry, however, had pushed out regular daily exercise for a few years. Over the previous nine months, my medical file had bulged considerably with two other health issues, one of which had culminated in a major (and very painful) operation three months prior. I'd also had a frightfully near miss coming back from a ministry trip when my car spun 720 degrees on black ice, slipped off the highway, and ended up on an embankment. Did these providences give me pause?

Not for long. That's why blood clots were required. God's message to me, through my blood, was: "*Stop!*"

My life and ministry had been getting faster and faster for years. It was all good stuff: delivering lectures, preaching sermons, counseling, speaking at conferences, writing books, raising four kids (now five), and so on. But it had been at the expense of quiet and rest—physical, emotional, mental, social, and spiritual rest. I hadn't neglected the means of grace—private devotions, family worship, and church attendance had all been steady and routine—but they were far too routine, with little or no joy in them. Life had become a restless, busy blur of ministry obligations and opportunities. The graces of sleep, exercise, peace, relaxation, a good diet, friendships, reflection, and fellowship with God had all been sacrificed for more "productive" activities. There had been little or no time to "Be still, and know that I am God" (Ps. 46:10).

But now, in the enforced stillness, I was hearing a loving and concerned God say, "My son, give me your heart" (Prov. 23:26). Not your sermons, not your lectures, not your blogs, not your books, not your meetings, but your heart. *You!*

It was not that I had been totally deaf to God's previous appeals and interventions. I had heard, and fully intended to respond. My plan had been to push through a jam-packed March and April, then use a four-week space in my calendar to get into better physical shape, return to healthier sleeping patterns, secure more time for rest, draw near to God, and renew fading friendships. That was my plan. And it was about to work. I'd just finished the last in a long series of speaking engagements and had settled down in my easy chair to begin my planned soul revival. And thirty minutes later, I was in a hospital. The Planner had swept my plan off the table.

Burnouts and Breakdowns

But why should I write all this? Why not just learn the lessons privately? I believe God gave me these experiences not only to teach *me*, but also to help *others* who have burned out or are about to. Since I began talking about this to many Christian men and at various Christian conferences, I've come across countless others who have suffered breakdowns or burnouts of one sort or another—some were physical like mine, but others were mental or relational breakdowns. Still others were emotional disorders or moral lapses. A number of men had not yet crashed and burned, but were worried about huge warning signs in their lives and wanted to do something to prevent impending disaster. One pastor confided: "My ministry had become a shell without the heart, a matter of endless duties without joy. I was standing up every Sunday telling God's people true things, good things. But they were no longer things that I lived on personally. It was my job."

Whatever the differences, whoever the person, whatever the problems, whatever the stage of stress or burnout, all saw that they were living at too fast a pace and needed to reset their lives. They wanted the grace of the gospel to be better reflected in the pace of their lives. They wanted more gospel joy in their service.

That prompted me to begin developing an informal program that I now call the Reset process. I have used it with numerous men, and now, through this book, I want to help you reset your life so that you can avoid crashing, or recover from it, by establishing patterns and rhythms that will help you live a grace-paced life and get you to the finish line successfully and joyfully.

This is not easy for most of us. We are independent, self-sufficient men who find it hard to admit weakness, seek help, and change deeply ingrained addictions to overwork, busyness, and productivity. For pastors and ministry leaders, it's especially difficult; since so much of our work is invisible and intangible, we can be tempted to go into overdrive in more noticeable tasks in order to prove that we are busy and strong. But it's also difficult because our work is more obviously gospel work. How can we back off? How can we slow the pace? How can we rest when there are souls to be saved and when the work is so inherently good and so (dangerously) enjoyable?

I've been there, and in some ways, I'm still there. It's still a daily battle for me to keep a safe pace. Changing lifelong patterns of thought, belief, and action can be extremely difficult. But it's worth fighting for a grace-paced life, not only because we will live longer (and therefore serve longer), but also because we will live more joyfully, fruitfully, and "grace-fully."

So I want to persuade you to a better and more useful life; but I also want to persuade you of the seriousness of your situation. The rest of this chapter will challenge you to take stock of your life, to have a sober look not just at the externals, but also at the internals—your heart and mind. This isn't mere self-centered navel-gazing. "Self-care is the first step in caring for others, for loving your neighbor as yourself,"[1] says J. R. Briggs. It's not selfish to replenish energy and renew vitality in order to serve God and others better. As one of my friends

---

1. J. R. Briggs, *Fail: Finding Hope and Grace in the Midst of Ministry Failure* (Downers Grove, IL: InterVarsity Press, 2014), Kindle edition, locs. 2082–2090.

reminded me, "Put your own oxygen mask on first, then you can help others." So, pull into Repair Bay 1, complete the checklist below, and use it to give yourself a reality check before reality checks you as it did me.

Reality Check

What should we be checking for? Our cars have warning lights that we can look up in our owner's manual. But what do the "warning lights" look like for men? What are the danger signs that our present pace may prematurely end our race? Here's a checklist arranged in categories. Whereas the physical category had the most ticks for me, for you it might be the emotional, mental, or another category. God has designed us all differently and knows which warning lights will best get our attention. But as some of us can't (or won't) see warning lights, even when all of them are flashing red and blue right in front of our eyes, why not ask your wife or a friend to go through these lights with you and give you a more objective outsider's viewpoint?

Physical Warning Lights

o You are suffering health issues one after another. Seventy-seven percent of Americans regularly experience physical symptoms caused by stress, including headaches, stomach cramps, achy joints, back pain, ulcers, breathlessness, bad skin, an irritable bowel, tremors, chest pains, or palpitations.[2]

o You feel exhausted and lethargic all the time, lacking energy or stamina for sports or playing with your kids.

---

2. "Stress Statistics," Statistic Brain website, October 19, 2015, http://www.statistic brain.com/stress-statistics/.

- You find it difficult to sleep, you wake up frequently, or you wake up early and can't get back to sleep. Maybe you can identify with my friend Paul's nightmare: "Then came the insomnia. Killer insomnia. Like all night. Then another night. I was panicking. What on earth was going on with me? I went to my doctor. He gave me some heavy-dose, prescription sleep aids. It worked like a peashooter on a tank."

- You are following the example of a young entrepreneur who admitted to me, "I used my lack of sleep to justify sleeping in later, which only perpetuated that poor sleep cycle."

- You are like one pastor who confessed to me that "my excessive sleeping was simply an escape."

- You are putting on weight through lack of exercise or eating too much junk food, or you are drinking too much alcohol or coffee.

Mental Warning Lights

- Concentration is hard; distraction is easy.

- You think obsessively about certain difficulties in your life. Jim described it to me like this: "Even little things began to fall on me with great weight. I would try to put them out of my mind, but it was like my brain was stuck. The thoughts kept spinning over and over. Nothing new was added to the process, no new solutions, no new information. Just the same cycle." Another man said it was like "trying to swat mental flies."

- You forget things you used to remember easily: appointments, birthdays, anniversaries, phone numbers, names, deadlines, etc.

o You find your attention drawn to negative subjects, and you are developing a hypercritical and cynical spirit.

o Your brain feels fried.

Emotional Warning Lights

o You feel sad, maybe so sad that you have bouts of weeping or feel you are on the verge of tears.

o It's been a long time since you had a good laugh or made someone laugh. Instead, there's emotional numbness.

o You feel pessimistic and hopeless about your marriage, children, church, job, nation, etc.

o Worry stalks your waking hours and anxiety climbs into bed with you every night.

o As soon as you wake and think about the day ahead, your heart starts pounding and your stomach starts churning over the decisions you face and people's expectations.

o You find it difficult to rejoice in others' joy, often forcing yourself to fake it.

o At times, you feel so hopeless and worthless that you think it would be better if you were not here.

Relational Warning Lights

o Your marriage is not what it once was. You don't delight in your wife as you once did.

o Your sex drive is erratic, as you often feel too tired to have anything but perfunctory, and mainly selfish, sex.

o You are irritable and snappy at your wife and children. They view you as angry, impatient, frustrated, and critical (ask them!).

○ You spend limited time with your children, and any time you do spend is interrupted by smartphone use or poisoned by thinking about all the other things you could be doing. A Christian friend admitted that he once started sobbing uncontrollably: "My startled wife asked what was wrong. I was watching my father-in-law play with my children and said to her, 'I wish I could enjoy them the way he does.' My own children had become a source of irritation. I envied him. I couldn't enjoy my own kids. I couldn't enjoy anything."

○ You avoid social occasions, neglect important relationships, and withdraw from friendships, even with people you care deeply about.

○ You frequently lose your temper and are in conflict with various people. One businessman told me that although he had rarely suffered through overwork, "as I have looked back over my life, the times that I have struggled with extended periods of depression have most often had in common that I was really struggling with a relationship. One time it was with my brother, twice it was a romantic relationship, twice it was struggles with my spouse."

Vocational Warning Lights

○ You work more than fifty hours per week, although not very efficiently, productively, or satisfyingly. As Greg McKeown puts it, "We have the unfulfilling experience of making a millimeter of progress in a million directions."[3]

---

3. Greg McKeown, *Essentialism: The Disciplined Pursuit of Less* (New York: The Crown Publishing Group, 2014), 7.

- Your work regularly spills over into evenings and weekends, or whatever days make up your "weekend."
- You have little joy in your work, you dread it, and you are so miserable that you would consider doing anything else but your present job. "I was confused," one pastor wrote to me, "and soon my confusion turned into bitterness toward God. 'What do you want from me? I work all the time. I have no hobbies, no down time, no joy, no life.' I began to hate the ministry."
- You are falling behind, feel constantly overwhelmed, and have begun to cut corners, take shortcuts, and drop your standards.
- Procrastination and indecision dominate as you flit from one thing to another to another with little sense of accomplishment. When you do make decisions, they are often the wrong ones.
- Motivation and drive have been replaced with avoidance, passivity, and apathy as you drag yourself through the day.
- You find it difficult to say no and feel like every woodpecker's favorite tree. One pastor admitted to me that he had reached the point where he hated being needed by so many people. He just wanted a regular job that he could leave behind after eight hours.
- You feel guilty or anxious when you are not working and regard yourself as lazy or weak for taking time off.

Moral Warning Lights

- You view risqué material on the Internet or have even "graduated" to using porn.
- You watch movies with language and images you'd never have tolerated in the past.

- Your expense account and tax return have some half-truths in them.
- You cultivate close relationships with women who are not your wife (or you think about it).
- You shade the truth in conversations, exaggerating or editing as appropriate.
- You medicate yourself (and your conscience) by over-spending, overdrinking, or overeating.

Spiritual Warning Lights

- Your personal devotions have decreased in length and increased in distraction, with little time or ability for meditation and reflection.
- You check email and social media before you meet with God each day.
- You don't have the same ongoing conversation with God that you used to have.
- You skip church.
- Listening to sermons sends you to sleep. One burnt-out businessman wrote to me, "One of the things that has been a great concern to me is the fact that I haven't been 'moved' by a sermon in years in spite of listening to some great sermons."
- You don't enjoy fellowship with other Christians or serving God's church.
- You believe all the truths of the Bible but you don't believe them for yourself.

Pastoral Warning Lights

- You are bored with the small stuff of ministry, thinking yourself above ministering to the seniors, the sick, and the time-wasters.

o After church, you don't hang around to fellowship with or minister to others.

o You are more taken up with the advancement of your own name than God's.

o You find it difficult to confess sin and even to admit weakness to God and others you are accountable to.

o You draw only on past knowledge and experience rather than present. As Aaron Armstrong put it: "We can rely on the backlog of information in our heads from years of reading, and not notice that something's wrong—that our metaphorical tanks are getting low—until we stop in the middle of traffic."[4]

o You base your acceptance by God on your hard work, your success, or your faithfulness. This painful story is too many pastors' experience: "When I felt like I was failing as a husband, father, pastor, Christian, even a human being, all I could do was work more, try harder. After all, there's no time for lollygagging when there's so much ground to regain. I made it impossible to rest. This made me a worse husband, father, pastor, Christian, and human being. That left me feeling more guilty."

What you're trying to do here is give yourself a reality check, to find out where you really are, how you really are, and who you really are. The next step is to analyze your checklist, to gauge the seriousness of these warning lights. You do that using three measurements:

How many? Probably everyone can tick a few of these items. That's life for fallen creatures in a fallen world. But if

---

4. Aaron Armstrong, "I've been running on empty—and what I'm doing to change that," *Blogging Theologically*, December 30, 2015, http://www.bloggingtheologically.com/2015/12/30/running-on-empty/.

you see five or more of these warning lights flashing on your dash, that should get your attention.

How deep? How serious are these issues? Rate the intensity of each of the ticks from one to five, with five being the most serious.

How long? How long has this been going on? The longer a symptom has lasted—especially if it has been a month or more—the more dangerous it is.

So you have your checklist and have analyzed it. It has a worrying number of ticks on problems that are sufficiently serious and that have been going on long enough for you to be concerned. What now?

First, you need to realize the danger you are in and the potential consequences if you don't slow down. As one of the men I've counseled put it: "One of the most important lessons I have had to learn is that if I don't slow down God will slow me down. And it's usually much more painful when he does it!"

Second, be grateful that God has alerted you to your danger before it is too late. Soul-weary pastor Josh Harris resigned from his church to go to seminary after a number of personal and ecclesiastical crises. He wrote: "I could keep grinding it out in ministry, but I knew that wouldn't be best for my soul, for my family, or for the church. I needed more than just a sabbatical—I needed significant retooling and recalibration. Time to stop talking and to listen. Time to relearn how to abide with Jesus. Time to unlearn professional busyness." But he resigned with thankfulness, as he explains: "If the way you're living isn't healthy—isn't expanding your soul and deepening your love for God and fellow-humans—then a crisis that awakens you to your need for change is a good thing. It's a God thing. And that's my experience."[5]

The good news is that there is a way back, a way to reset your life, get all of these dimensions back on track, and start enjoying a grace-paced life. That's what this book is about. Let me give you a brief summary of what you can expect in the following chapters in order to encourage you to proceed.

You've already passed through Repair Bay 1—"Reality Check." In the next chapter, you'll reverse into Repair Bay 2, "Review," to figure out how you got here, what caused these various issues. It's important to understand causes so that you can avoid repeating the same mistakes a few years down the road.

Then you'll circle around through eight more repair bays as you perform a step-by-step reset of your life. Some of these bays will be more relevant and applicable to you than others. But it's worth reading about each of them just in case you miss something crucial. It will also help you to help others. These chapters will be characterized by:

Practicality. Most men are solution-focused, and that's what I want this book to be. I'll keep theory to a minimum, offering just enough to help you understand the practical steps you have to take.

Sympathy. I told you my own story (and I'll tell you more of it) partly to show you I'm not writing this from the new-car showroom. I'm writing this as someone who has crashed, burned, and ended up in the wrecker's yard. I understand and I sympathize, as do the other men whose stories appear in

---

5. Josh Harris, "The 40-Year-Old Seminarian," *Christianity Today*, December 4, 2015, http://www.christianitytoday.com/le/2015/fall/40-year-old-seminarian.html.

these pages.[6] I understand how difficult it is to reset our lives after years of unhealthy patterns and rhythms. I'm not writing this as a success story but as the account of a fellow struggler.

Hope. Whatever place you find yourself in, your life can be reset and you can find a more joyful and sustainable pace to help you enjoy and finish your race.

Joy. Although you've been through or are in various kinds of pain, and although some parts of the repair process may be a bit painful initially, the ultimate aim is the restoration of joy. That's why the last repair bay is called "Resurrection." That's not just an end-of-life doctrine; by God's grace, it can also become an everyday life experience. We can know the power of Christ's resurrection daily raising us up from the dark depths of sin, stress, anxiety, burnout, depression, strife, and backsliding, and renewing our lives.

Two Questions

After my near-fatal crash, two questions kept bugging me: "Where is God in all this?" and "What is he doing?" I was doing God's work, I was sacrificing myself for the kingdom, I was spending and being spent for Christ, and it landed me in the ER and almost in a coffin. Where is God and what is he doing? Initially, my best answers to these two questions were, "I do not know" and "I do not know."

Then, in the midst of my puzzling, I remembered that an even greater sufferer (and a far godlier man than I) also had asked these questions as he looked back down the rocky road of life (Job 23:1–9). "Where's God? And what's he doing?" Thankfully, Job came up with far better answers than I did.

---

6. Names have been changed to protect privacy.

God knows where I am. "He knows the way that I take" (23:10a). Although we don't know where God is and we may not even know where *we* are, God knows our exact location, direction, and destination. Just like a child on a long car journey, we don't need to know where we are as long as Dad knows.

God knows what he's doing. "When He has tested me, I shall come forth as gold" (23:10b). He's not just proving us but improving us. With his hand on the thermostat and his eye on the timer, he knows exactly how hot the furnace needs to be and how long to leave us in it to make our gold purer and brighter.

God knows where we are and he knows what he's doing! The end product is gold, especially the gold of a closer relationship with God and of greater usefulness to others. Hold on to these priceless answers as we drive into the second repair bay.

Review

We're men. We're practical. We like to do things. We've just spent a chapter coming to grips with the damage we've suffered, and now we want to fix it. We want something to do. "Let's get started on the repairs!"

Slooooow down. We need to spend one more chapter on knowing and understanding before we get to the fixing. We've done damage assessment; now we need to shift into reverse and look back at what caused that damage. If we don't, we may well get fixed up, but later go out and do exactly the same things that put us in the garage in the first place.

That's what I did. Three years after my blood-clot drama, I ended up back in the ER to hear the doctor say, "They're back!" Blood clots had splattered my lungs again, this time with no prior leg pain to warn me. Tears immediately filled my eyes, not so much from the physical pain, but from the mental and spiritual pain of knowing that I had failed to learn the lessons my heavenly Father had been patiently pounding into my thick skull. Instead, I had thoughtlessly and presumptuously returned to the dangerous pace of life that had put me in the hospital before. I also wept with joy and relief that God had given me yet another chance to learn. I was somewhat comforted by one Christian who told me that he also had needed multiple setbacks before he finally made the changes that led to lasting change. But I now knew I had to get far more serious about this resetting and go far deeper into the causes of my suicidal lifestyle. I had to ask myself the same questions that Bill Hybels wrestled with when he had his "ER moment" in a grocery store parking lot: "How did this happen? How did I become this overwhelmed, overscheduled, exhausted person who is devoid of compassion and angry at everybody? How did this happen?"[1]

So before we lift the hood and get down to the nuts and bolts, we need to take a big-picture look at our humanity in order to understand the interaction between our bodies, our minds, and our souls.

Think about how the different parts of our cars interact. They don't work independently, but each part depends upon and is affected by the others. If we put bad fuel in our cars, it really doesn't matter how many cylinders they have or how good their tires are. Similarly, we have to understand how one part of our being affects the others. So let's look a bit deeper into what kind of creatures God has made us to be.

We Are God's Creatures

Many of our problems happen not only because we do the wrong things, but also because we believe the wrong things. Behind many seemingly practical problems are theological

---

1. Bill Hybels, *Simplify: Ten Practices to Unclutter Your Soul* (Carol Stream, IL: Tyndale Momentum, 2014), 10.

problems. At the root of many of the issues we identified in chapter 1 is a wrong view of God. And it's not just a slightly wrong view; it's a fundamental and foundational error, because it concerns the fundamental and foundational truth that *God is our Creator*. That's the very first truth revealed to us in Scripture. And it's first for a reason: if we go wrong there, we run a great risk of going wrong everywhere else. Forgetting we are Christians has serious consequences, but so does forgetting we are human.

Now, some of you are thinking: "Don't insult me. I believe in God as Creator. I defend God as Creator. I fight those who deny God as Creator. I can even prove God is Creator. How can you say that my problems arise from denying God as Creator?"

Well, maybe we are not denying God as Creator with our lips, but some of us are doing so with our lives.

Creationists Living like Evolutionists

Lots of people call God *Creator* but live like evolutionists. It's as if life is about the survival of the fittest rather than about living like a dependent creature—trusting our Creator rather than ourselves—and according to our Maker's instructions.

How would you feel if you built a remote-control model car for your children, only to come home a few days later to hear that they had broken it by trying to use it as a plane? You'd say, "I gave you a car, and I gave you car instructions; why did you ignore them and treat the car like a plane?" Similarly, God has given us instructions about how to live as his creatures, as the finite body-and-soul beings he has made us to be. But some of us are trying to live as if we are infinite. It's hardly surprising that we are breaking down.

Retired pastor Al Martin told me that he was frequently contacted by young pastors he had trained who were just months into their ministries. They would say: "Help, Pastor Martin! I can't pray, I can't study, I can't sleep, I can't go on. I think I'm going to have to resign."

"Here's your problem," Pastor Martin would calmly reply. "You're trying to live like a disembodied angel rather than flesh-and-blood humanity. Here's your solution: first, exercise vigorously three times a week. Second, take one full day off a week. And third, spend at least one evening a week with your wife."

"But Pastor Martin, I can't do that. There are souls to be saved, people need my counsel, I don't have enough time as it is . . ."

Pastor Martin would wait patiently until the familiar excuses and defenses ran out before firmly closing the conversation by saying: "You called me for advice, right? Well, do these three things and call me back within the next month if they don't work." He said he's never been called back.

Word and World

God publishes his instructions about how we are to live as dependent, finite creatures in two places: his Word and his world. By "his Word" I mean the Bible, which contains general principles, specific instructions, and relevant examples—all of which will be of enormous help to us in this repair-and-reset process. By "his world" I mean the physical world in which we live, from study of which God has enabled scientists to learn about how the body and the mind function best. For example, I recently saw research that was headlined, "The more you sit, the sooner you will die!" That made me sit up.

In truth, it made me stand up! That's my loving Creator's instruction coming to me via reliable research, which I read through the spectacles of Scripture to make sure I let in only what agrees with God's Word.

We'll do quite a lot of that in this garage. To live a grace-paced life, we will need every grace-provided truth. We will gather our Creator's gracious instructions from wherever he has placed them, but we will use God's Word to read God's world.

We Are Complex Creatures

We are not just body and we are not just soul; we are body and soul united in one person. Our bodies are composed of millions of atoms, with 90 percent of them replaced every year. We are a complex mix of physical materials and physical forces—electricity, chemicals, plumbing, gasses, pumps, siphons, lubrication, buttons, switches, receptors, and so on.

Our souls are even more complex than our bodies and totally inaccessible to empirical research. Although the Bible gives us some basic data about the soul, much remains a mystery. And when we unite a complex body and a complex soul in one person, we get multiple complexities!

The interconnectivity of the physical and the spiritual means that the health of the body affects the health of the soul and vice versa, and it's not always easy to figure out the contribution of each to our problems! But we cannot neglect one realm and expect the other not to suffer the consequences (Prov. 17:22; Ps. 32:3–4).

For example, one of my friends went through a dark period of doubting his salvation and sought in vain for a spiritual cause. He repented and repented; he repented of his repentance; and he repented of what he had not repented of. Darkness still enveloped his soul. Slowly and reluctantly, he accepted the counsel that he had been overworking for too long and carrying the crushing burden of too many problems of too many people. He started to build quiet and peace into his life, and began to delegate some of his problems to others. Soon the light began to dawn and assurance gradually returned to his soul.

It's not just the physical that affects the spiritual; it goes the other way as well. One pastor I know went through a discouraging period of ill health. His doctor couldn't find anything wrong. In one of our conversations, it emerged that he had been nursing jealousy against another pastor for many years. He had grown resentful of that man's success, wishing it were his own. As he confessed this sin, and as he slowly rebuilt his sense of identity independent of the other pastor and rooted in Christ alone, his various illnesses cleared up. We are complex creatures.

We Are Limited Creatures

Creatures, by definition, are less than their Creator. He is infinite, we are finite; he is unlimited, we are limited. Although none of us would say we are unlimited, most of us think we are less limited than we actually are.

Such underestimating of our limitations and overestimating of our abilities results inevitably in strain, fraying, and eventually breaking. Try it with anything—a car engine, a towrope, a computer, a bridge. Underestimate their limitations and overestimate their abilities, and you will eventually blow the engine, break the rope, crash the computer, and collapse the bridge. Why do we think it's any different with ourselves? Sure, we can operate at exceptional levels for a short time, but sooner or later, our limits have to be faced. Verses like Philippians 4:13—"I can do all things through Christ who strengthens me"—do not override our basic need to eat, drink, rest, and sleep.

How can we find out our personal limits, though? I regularly back up into Repair Bay 1 for an inspection. If two or three of those warning lights are on, I'm not too worried. That's just life. But if five or more are on, or if even one of them is on in the moral or spiritual categories, then I know I'm exceeding safe limits and must take urgent action.

We Are Fallen Creatures

Like all fishermen, I'm fatally attracted to the latest "guaranteed" fish-catching reel. As we all know, the more complicated (and expensive) a reel is, the more likely it is to catch fish. Right? Now, complicated reels are great when they are working well, but when they break down, they make a much bigger mess than standard reels.

That's why humanity is in a much worse state than any other creature; the more complex the creature, the more mess when they break. And what a mess sin and death have caused! Our bodies, our minds, our chemistry, our physics, our plumbing, our electrics; everything is in such a mess—each part of our humanity on its own and especially each faulty part as it interacts with other faulty parts.

But the best news is that our gracious and powerful Creator is in the business of re-creating, a process that requires our cooperation and that we hinder if we do not live within the limits of our createdness and fallenness.

How Did I Get Here?

We've spent quite a bit of time on the interconnection and interaction of various parts of our humanity in order to avoid simplistic spiritual-only or physical-only approaches to our problems. But now let's get down to specific causes of our problems. When we reverse back down the road of life, what do we see that has damaged us along the way?

Most causes can be placed into one of two main categories—our life situation and our lifestyle. Although the damage usually results from a mixture of factors in both categories, and life-situation problems often produce lifestyle problems (and vice versa), sometimes it is only life situation or only lifestyle factors. But how do we know for sure?

That's where my wife, Shona, is such a great help to me. When I'm down, I tend to either blame everything but myself or else see myself as to blame for everything and take responsibility for things that are outside my control. Shona brings more of an outsider's view, resulting in greater objectivity and accuracy. From time to time, I've also sought an objective assessment of my life situation and lifestyle from a trusted friend, a colleague at work, or a wise elder. Whomever you choose, you must be sure that he or she will be totally honest with you. Be cautious about seeking advice from someone who stands to lose if you need to slow down.

Life Situation

Our "life situation" refers to things that we have little or no choice about or control over. Life happens. Stuff happens. From my own experience, and from what I've come across in counseling others, the most common of these situational factors are:

Illness. As we saw in Repair Bay 1, illness can be the result of burnout. But it can also be a cause. The degree to which illnesses impact us depends on the nature, number, severity, and duration of those illnesses.

Genes. Research has found that our genes explain about 50 percent of our happiness or lack of it.[2] Although that's probably overstating the case, it helps explain my own experience in counseling depressed Christians, the majority of whom have at least one parent who suffered with depression.

Caregiving. Someone close to me suffered all-over body pain for a number of years. Multiple tests could find nothing wrong. Painkillers had limited success. He thought he was going to have to live with this for the rest of his days. Some years later, the elderly relative he had been caring for in his own home for a number of years passed away. Within a few weeks, his pain was gone! There's a cost to caring.

Bereavement. Again, there is a range of pain here, depending on the nature of the relationship, the way the person died, and the proximity of other bereavements.

Loss. It might be the loss of a job, a friendship, a home, money, your reputation, or a ministry. Maybe you've lost possessions through theft or been the victim of another type of crime. Another painful loss one Christian young man asked me to point out is the loss of sex. At various points in his marriage, his wife lost all interest in sex, the lack of which, he said, directly impacted his stress levels and sleep patterns.

Gain. Gains can stress us as much as losses. Promotion often results in longer hours, greater responsibility, and

2. S. Lyubomirsky, K. M. Sheldon, and D. Schkade, "Pursuing Happiness: The Architecture of Sustainable Change," *Review of General Psychology* 9 (2005): 111–31.

increased anxiety about learning new tasks, working with a new team, and so on.

Moving. The stress of relocation takes a bigger toll than we realize, especially when it is involuntary. It may also be accompanied by a loss of social support from extended family members. One friend, Joe, who's moved a lot over the years, spoke to me about what he and his wife have called "post-traumatic moving syndrome."

Conflict. Few things drain me as much as conflict; not just those I end up in, but also those I'm asked to mediate. Then there are church conflicts and splits. I'd rather go into the ring with Mike Tyson; at least I'd soon be unconscious.

Backsliding (of others). In my early Christian life, I was body-slammed when my spiritual hero, used in my conversion and call to the ministry, was revealed as an immoral man. I lost fifteen pounds over the course of two years because of the stress of it all.

Injustice. As Asaph found out, the prosperity of the wicked and the suffering of the righteous can knock us off our feet (Psalm 73).

Evil. The media pours the gloomiest news from every part of the nation and the world into our eyes and ears. It is so wearing and wearying. Entrepreneur Charlie Hoehn, the author of *Play It Away*, found that when he cut the news out of his life completely, his anxiety plummeted within two weeks.[3]

Sorrow overload. Pastors especially suffer with this as they deal daily with some of the most excruciating problems of life. At times, these can overwhelm us, especially when Facebook brings the sorrows of innumerable others we hardly know into

---

3. Charlie Hoehn, *Play It Away: A Workaholic's Cure for Anxiety* (CharlieHoehn .com, 2014), Kindle edition, loc. 559.

our lives, exhausting our compassion reserves. "I can develop a sort of emotional hypochondria," one pastor told me, "taking on too much personal stress from the problems of others."

Responsibility. We get married, we have children, we are promoted, we serve a church, our congregation grows, and so on. Each of these changes adds more and more responsibility to our lives, raising our RPM, wearing and tearing our engines, and draining precious fuel.

Aging. In our twenties and thirties, we can handle the growing responsibilities of life, but often in our early forties, we begin to creak and crack as age begins to weaken our bodies and minds. We may not yet be "over the hill," but we're definitely slowing and fraying as we reach the top of it.

Bad examples. We are deeply and often unconsciously affected by the examples of our parents. Overly critical, excessively negative, extremely competitive, or conflict-ridden home environments can cast dark shadows over our whole lives.

Differences. We all have different capacities and limitations, largely determined by our genes. We must not allow others' limits to become our own, as they have different thresholds in different areas of their lives.

Change. Global and local change is happening at unprecedented and exponential rates, creating a climate of tremendous uncertainty. Margin expert Richard Swenson warns: "No one in the history of humankind has ever had to live with the number and intensity of stressors we have acting upon us today. They are unprecedented. The human spirit is called upon to withstand rapid changes and pressures never before encountered."[4]

---

4. Richard Swenson, *Margin: Restoring Emotional, Physical, Financial, and Time Reserves to Overloaded Lives* (Colorado Springs: NavPress, 2004), 46.

Blessing. Seasons of blessing in a church's life often result in pastors, elders, and others having an increased workload of counseling and discipleship, as well as a host of new problems to deal with from the lives of new converts.

Sovereignty. God may permit us to fall into depression or anxiety for no apparent reason. There is no human explanation, just divine sovereignty. That causes its own struggles, as this Christian man discovered:

> I couldn't burn out! I was doing so much right! I had a very healthy marriage, a great love life. I never looked at porn. I read the Bible and prayed daily. I didn't cheat my family either—I played with my kids for an hour most every night. I had an annual spiritual "checkup" with a seasoned pastor I respected. But there I was. I was having a genuine, certified, 14-karat breakdown. Full stop.

Although these are all life events over which we have little or no control, we are responsible for our reactions to them. Our responses can make some situations, or their impact upon us, better or worse.

Lifestyle

Now we want to move on to look at lifestyle factors for which we do have a choice, things that we can largely control. The most common causes of damage here are:

Idolatry. In men, this is often manifested in the worship of work—the setting up of our vocations and careers as our gods, the sources of our ultimate joy and satisfaction. God put a special curse on men's work (Gen. 3:17–19) to make sure that our idolizing of work would never fully satisfy.

Greed. Often related to the idolizing of work is the greedy pursuit of money and other material rewards, which causes so many to work so long and sleep so little.

Debt. No matter how hard we work and how much we earn, we keep living beyond our means, gradually accumulating more and more debt, and more and more anxiety.

People pleasing. We do everything we can to earn the praise of our parents, our wives, our bosses, our friends, or, if we are pastors, our congregations. In a plea for much greater honesty and transparency among pastors, Matt wrote: "I lived in constant shame for how enslaved I was to what people thought of me. I hated it but couldn't seem to let it go. To make matters worse, no one around me was talking about it. It didn't seem like a problem for anyone else. I felt pathetic and alone."

Perfectionism. Sometimes we can impose far too high standards upon ourselves, which either paralyzes us or sends us into a frenzy of activity. A fellow seminarian of mine wouldn't spend less than thirty hours on a sermon, polishing and polishing it until it was "perfect." Not surprisingly, he burned out and left the ministry within a year.

Pride. Even in ministry, it's much too easy to build our own kingdoms instead of God's, promoting our names rather than his. As one pastor wrote: "Why am I nervous to admit that I can't do everything that needs to be done? I think it's simple. I am afraid to confess that I have limits. I'm afraid to admit that I have God-allotted periods and boundaries of my dwelling place (Acts 17:26). And I'm afraid that will render me unimportant."[5]

Comparison. A pastor friend described how much he

---

5. Brad Andrews, "Limitless Grace for Limited Leaders," *For the Church*, February 29, 2016, http://ftc.co/resource-library/1/1933.

struggled with comparing himself and his church to other pastors and churches:

> I would hear of another pastor friend with all kinds of people in his church, having babies upon babies. I can count on one hand the babies I've baptized. They've had conversions. I've had one—and not even in my own congregation. What was I doing wrong? Why could another man work less in evangelism with more results, while I had to knock my head on a wall for next to nothing?

Enjoyment. Some of us—especially pastors—enjoy our work so much that we have to exercise self-denial lest what is good become harmful to us.

Indiscipline. Disorganization, procrastination, addiction to technology, or refusal to do unpleasant duties tends to stress us more than diligence, organization, decisiveness, or self-denial.

Identity. Defining who we are by our work or our social media profiles bases our self-worth upon our vocational success or the number of likes or followers we can attract, neither of which are stable or healthy. In "The 'Busy' Trap," Tim Kreider wrote, "Busyness serves as a kind of existential reassurance, a hedge against emptiness; obviously your life cannot possibly be silly or trivial or meaningless if you are so busy, completely booked, in demand every hour of the day."[6]

Unbelief. Living as if there were no God, or as if there were no God who cares for us far more than for the carefree sparrows (Matt. 6:26), cannot but produce angst and inner turmoil.

Diet. We are what we eat. Many studies have demonstrated the impact of our food upon our mood. If you don't believe

---

6. Tim Kreider, "The 'Busy' Trap," *The New York Times*, June 30, 2012, http://opinionator.blogs.nytimes.com/2012/06/30/the-busy-trap/.

that, eat nothing but junk food for the next seven days. Or, better, ask a diabetic about how blood-sugar levels affect his cognitive abilities and emotions.

Media diet. Just as above, we are what we consume. Many of us live as if Philippians 4:8 says, "Whatever things are false, whatever things are sordid, whatever things are wrong, whatever things are filthy, whatever things are ugly, whatever things are terrible, if there is any vice and if there is anything worthy of criticism—meditate on these things."

Laziness. We do not exercise the bodies God has given us to steward, allowing them to become stiff, weak, flabby, and overweight, with unintended consequences for our thinking, feeling, and willing.

Failure. We make bad choices, we fail at jobs, we don't rise to our own or others' expectations, our congregations decline rather than grow.

Conscience. Living with a guilty conscience over unconfessed and unforsaken sin is not much of a life. Whoever covers sin cannot prosper (Prov. 28:13). David made himself physically sick through it (Ps. 32:3–5). But living with *false* guilt can also drain us.

Backsliding. In some ways, all of the above is backsliding, but I'm thinking here especially of the gradual loss of contact with God through regularly rushed or missed daily devotions, or of the life lived independently of God, resulting in a growing distance between us and God, and a growing proximity to temptation and sin.

Straws and Hammers

There are other life events and lifestyle issues we could add to these lists, but use these as a sampler to review your life.

Don't brush off or minimize any of them, because, although there may not be one *big* cause you can identify, for many people, it's an accumulation of lots of little things that eventually breaks them. For others, it may be one small thing that comes at the end of many big things. Or maybe it's a few huge sucker-punches in a row, as in the case of my friend Dan: "Through my wife's stage-four cancer, a church merger, a grave sin of a highly regarded mentor, and a personal trauma one of my children experienced, I had accumulated a great deal of unrelieved stress."

We are all different: we have different limits and different vulnerabilities. As one man said to me, "The straw that broke the camel's back came at the end of many hammer-blows on the same back."

So we have assessed the damage and understood the causes of it. We have begun to admit the harm we do to ourselves when we live a space-age-paced life rather than a grace-paced life. Let's now get on to the more practical and positive parts of this book as we maneuver into the third repair bay —"Rest."

Rest

If you awoke one morning in a pool of blood, you'd probably change your life.

That's what happened to Arianna Huffington, of *Huffington Post* fame, after she collapsed from exhaustion and smashed her cheekbone on her desk as she dropped to the floor. She was at the peak of her success, with money and power in abundance, but something was not right. As she said in her bestselling book, *Thrive*: "I was not living a successful life by any sane definition of success. I knew something had to radically change. I could not go on that way."[1] And change she did, especially in the area of sleeping more, so much so that she sometimes describes herself as a sleep evangelist. She certainly converted me, and, as a new sleep proselyte, I hope I can also convert you to a healthier and humbler sleep style.

In a BBC article headlined "'Arrogance' of Ignoring Need

---

1. Arianna Huffington, *Thrive: The Third Metric to Redefining Success and Creating a Life of Well-Being, Wisdom, and Wonder* (New York: Harmony, 2015), 2.

for Sleep,"[2] leading scientists warned of the supreme arrogance of trying to do without sufficient sleep. They discovered that we are sleeping between one and two hours less per night than people did sixty or so years ago, and two and a half hours less than a hundred years ago, and it's having a devastating impact upon every part of our lives. Yet when was the last time you heard a sermon on sleep? We spend about 30 percent of our lives doing it, and nothing impacts our lives more than doing it, yet, from the pulpit, we hear only crickets. Have Christians mastered sleep so well that we don't need instruction on it?

Maybe you're thinking: "Instruction on sleep? Are you serious? Is it that complicated? You close your eyes. Darkness. You open your eyes. Light. What's to learn?" Much more than you probably realize!

In previous *Reset* bays, we assessed the damage and reviewed the causes. Now we're moving into the repair stage, and it begins with getting into bed. Yes, a grace-paced life begins with stopping and accepting the grace of sleep. Many men think they can skip this bay, but those who do so end up spending much longer in the garage, and some never exit.

The Sermon We Preach in Our Sleep

Few things are as theological as sleep. Show me your sleep pattern and I'll show you your theology, because we all preach a sermon in and by our sleep. For example, if we pride ourselves on sleeping only five hours a night, we preach the following truths:

I don't trust God with my work, my church, or my family. Sure, I believe God is sovereign, but he needs all the help I

---

2. James Gallagher, "'Arrogance' of Ignoring Need for Sleep," BBC, May 12, 2014, http://www.bbc.com/news/health-27286872.

can give him. If I don't do the work, who will? Although Christ has promised to build his church, who's doing the night shift?

I don't respect how my Creator has made me. I am strong enough to cope without God's gift of sufficient daily sleep (Ps. 3:5; 4:8). I refuse to accept my creaturely limitations and bodily needs (Ps. 127:1–2). I see myself more as a machine than a human being.

I don't believe that the soul and body are linked. I can neglect my body and my soul will not suffer. I can weaken my body and not weaken my mind, conscience, and will.

I don't need to demonstrate my rest in Christ. Although the Bible repeatedly portrays salvation as rest, I'll let others do the resting. I want people to know how busy, important, and zealous I am. That's far more important than the daily demonstration of Christ's salvation in when and how I rest.

I worship idols. What I do instead of sleep shines a spotlight on my idols, whether it be late-night football, surfing the Internet, ministry success, or promotion. Why sleep when it does nothing to burnish my reputation or advance my glory?

What sermon are you preaching in your sleep?

Multiple Good Reasons to Sleep Longer

Before we discuss how to sleep better and longer, consider some of the devastating consequences of reduced sleep. Or, to put it more positively, here are multiple good reasons to sleep longer.

Physical Consequences
Numerous studies have warned about the long-term results of chronic sleep deprivation (averaging less than six hours

a night). Just one week of sleeping fewer than six hours a night results in damaging changes to more than seven hundred genes, coronary narrowing, and signs of brain tissue loss.[3] The latter is partly because sleep activates the brain's garbage disposal system, cleaning out toxins and waste products.[4] Chronic sleep deprivation is associated with increased risk of infection, stroke, cancer, high blood pressure, heart disease, and infertility. Sleep loss increases hunger, desire for larger portion sizes, and preference for high-calorie, high-carb foods, with the resulting risk of obesity.[5] In short, sleeping is not a useless waste of time, but an essential biological need that prevents infection and helps us maintain healthy body weight.

Sporting Consequences

The physical consequences of too little sleep can be even better understood and appreciated when we examine sports science and learn why more and more elite athletes are increasing sleep and even hiring sleep coaches in order to improve their performance. Two days of sleep reduction lead to a more than 20 percent reduction in attention spans, reaction times, strength, stamina, accuracy, and speed.

It is little wonder that the average sleep time of top athletes is well above average.[6] Tennis champion Roger Federer sleeps

3. Many of the statistics and quotations for this section come from *Sleep Disorders and Sleep Deprivation: An Unmet Public Health Problem* (Washington DC: National Academies Press, 2006).

4. L. Xie et al., "Sleep drives metabolite clearance from the adult brain," National Center for Biotechnology Information, October 18, 2013, http://www.ncbi.nlm.nih.gov /pubmed/24136970.

5. Christine Gorman, "Why We Sleep," *Scientific American*, October 1, 2015, http:// www.scientificamerican.com/article/sleep-why-we-sleep-video/.

6. The following statistics and quotations come from "You Are What You Sleep," *Athlete Kinetics*, February 9, 2016, https://blog.athletekinetics.com/2016/02/09/you-are -what-you-sleep/ and Jordan Schultz, "These Famous Athletes Rely on Sleep for Peak

eleven to twelve hours per night, sprinter Usain Bolt eight to ten hours, basketball star Lebron James twelve hours, and tennis champion Rafael Nadal eight to nine hours. Then there's golfer Tiger Woods at five hours, which might explain a lot! Former NBA star Grant Hill said, "I think sleep is just as important as diet and exercise." Federer explained, "If I don't sleep 11–12 hours a day, it's not right."

Intellectual Consequences

"Yeah, but I'm no Roger Federer," you say. "I just sit at a computer all day. I don't need to perform at such a high physical level." True, but sleep is equally important for knowledge workers. In "Sleep Is More Important than Food," Tony Schwartz says the research is unanimous—the better you sleep, the more you learn:

> Even small amounts of sleep deprivation take a significant toll on our health, our mood, our cognitive capacity and our productivity. . . . Many of the effects we suffer are invisible. Insufficient sleep, for example, deeply impairs our ability to consolidate and stabilize learning that occurs during the waking day. In other words, it wreaks havoc on our memory.[7]

A study from Luebeck University in Germany found that twice as many of those who slept for eight hours solved a problem compared to those whose sleep was interrupted.[8] The

---

Performance," *The Huffington Post*, August 13, 2014, http://www.huffingtonpost.com /2014/08/13/these-famous-athletes-rely-on-sleep_n_5659345.html.

7. Tony Schwartz, "Sleep Is More Important than Food," *Harvard Business Review*, March 3, 2011, https://hbr.org/2011/03/sleep-is-more-important-than-f.html.

8. Ullrich Wagner et al., "Sleep Inspires Insight," *Nature* 427 (Jan. 22, 2004): 352–55, www.nature.com/nature/journal/v427/n6972/full/nature02223.html. An additional study supports the idea: Michael Hopkin, "Sleep Boosts Lateral Thinking," *Nature*, January 22, 2004, www.nature.com/news/2004/040122/full/news040119-10.html.

researchers concluded that it wasn't just that they were better rested, but that their brains had been physically renewed overnight, making new neural connections so they could achieve more in less time.

Emotional Consequences

By sleeping less and working more, the *quantity* of our work may increase in the short term, but the *quality* definitely decreases, and so does our enjoyment of what we do. That's because sleep loss disrupts the brain's flow of epinephrine, dopamine, and serotonin, chemicals closely associated with mood and behavior. Thus, people with insomnia are ten times as likely to develop depression and seventeen times as likely to have significant anxiety. Studies led by Torbjörn Åkerstedt of Stockholm University found that less sleep reduces empathy levels but increases fear levels.[9] In *Play It Away*, Charlie Hoehn writes:

> Every anxious person I've met has either been in denial about how little sleep they get, or they're overlooking the fact that they're going to bed at random hours every night. One of my readers wrote this message to me after reviewing an early draft of this chapter: "When I began forcing myself to sleep eight hours a night, my physical health problems cleared up, my emotions balanced out, and my anxiety disappeared. My mind could function and that tight feeling around my eyes vanished. Eight hours of sleep is a miracle pill."[10]

---

9. See a summary of Åkerstedt's research at Karolinska Institutet, Department of Clinical Neuroscience, http://ki.se/en/cns/torbjorn-akerstedts-research-group.

10. Charlie Hoehn, *Play It Away: A Workaholic's Cure for Anxiety* (CharlieHoehn. com, 2014), Kindle edition, locs. 1081–89.

Societal Consequences

Question: Which of the Ten Commandments can you keep in your sleep? Answer: The sixth commandment, "You shall not murder" (Ex. 20:13), because, as the following statistics demonstrate, getting enough sleep is an act of loving your neighbor.

The cognitive impairment that results from being awake for twenty-four hours is higher than the drunken-driving limit in all states. According to the National Highway Traffic Safety Administration, falling asleep while driving is responsible for at least one hundred thousand crashes, seventy-one thousand injuries, and 1,550 deaths each year in the United States.[11] Disasters such as the *Exxon Valdez* oil spill, the *Challenger* space shuttle explosion, and the Metro North train crash in New York were all linked to sleep deprivation.

On a more mundane level, I notice (and so does my family) that I am much more irritable, bad-tempered, and likely to end up in conflict when I've skimped on sleep. No amount of productivity is worth that damage to precious relationships.

Financial Consequences

Because it undermines safety, creativity, problem-solving ability, and productivity, too little sleep is estimated to cost American businesses $63 billion a year. Studies have shown that customers and clients are likely to register a sleep-deprived salesperson as unhealthy and lacking energy, reducing sales.

Also, despite caricatures to the contrary, many entrepreneurs have built their success on sleep. Jeff Bezos of Amazon said: "I'm more alert and I think more clearly. I just feel so

---

11. "Drowsy Driving and Automobile Crashes," *NCSDR/NHTSA Expert Panel on Driver Fatigue and Sleepiness*, http://www.nhtsa.gov/people/injury/drowsy_driving1/Drowsy.html.

much better all day long if I've had eight hours." Although Netscape co-founder Mark Andressen used to skimp on sleep, he learned: "Seven [hours] and I start to degrade. Six is suboptimal. Five is a big problem. Four means I'm a zombie."[12]

Moral Consequences

Studies show that a lack of sleep depletes and weakens the brain's self-control center, leading to higher levels of unethical behavior. In one study of whether people would cheat or not given identical temptations, those in the group that did not cheat were found to have slept on average about twenty-two minutes more than those who cheated. The difference between moral and immoral actions was only twenty-two minutes of sleep! Former U.S. President Bill Clinton once said that every major mistake he had ever made coincided with sleep deprivation. If that doesn't make you sleep longer, nothing will.

One man who came to me for counseling after being convicted of driving under the influence of alcohol admitted that he was sleeping only three to four hours a night and drinking more and more each week. Once he increased his sleep, his desire for alcohol decreased.

Spiritual Consequences

But it's more than morality that's at stake; it's also our spirituality. Ponder this paragraph from Don Carson:

> If you are among those who become nasty, cynical, or even full of doubt when you are missing your sleep, you are morally obligated to try to get the sleep you need. We

---

12. Nancy Jeffrey, "Sleep Is the New Status Symbol for Successful Entrepreneurs," *The Wall Street Journal*, April 2, 1999, http://online.wsj.com/article/SB923008887262090895.html.

are whole, complicated beings; our physical existence is tied to our spiritual well-being, to our mental outlook, to our relationships with others, including our relationship with God. Sometimes the godliest thing you can do in the universe is get a good night's sleep—not pray all night, but sleep. I'm certainly not denying that there may be a place for praying all night; I'm merely insisting that in the normal course of things, spiritual discipline obligates you get the sleep your body needs.[13]

Ministry Consequences

Unsurprisingly, all the damage outlined above inevitably leads to ministry fallout too. A pastor shared with me that he had been raised and trained to think that "if we punish or neglect our bodies in the service of the kingdom, God will magically override any negative consequences." He warned, "We may not realize we are believing this until he lets the consequences materialize and we act confused or bitter toward God."

When lecturing about Charles Spurgeon's suffering with depression, John Piper said:

I am emotionally less resilient when I lose sleep. There were early days when I would work without regard to sleep and feel energized and motivated. In the last seven or eight years my threshold for despondency is much lower. For me, adequate sleep is not a matter of staying healthy. It is a matter of staying in the ministry. It is irrational that my future should look bleaker when I get four or five hours sleep several nights in a row. But that is irrelevant.

13. Don Carson, *Scandalous: The Cross and Resurrection of Jesus* (Wheaton, IL: Crossway, 2010), 147.

Those are the facts. And I must live within the limits of facts. I commend sufficient sleep to you, for the sake of your proper assessment of God and his promises.[14]

Did you notice how Piper connected time on the pillow with trust in God's promises?

A Few Sleeping Pills

By now, I hope you're begging for help to sleep better. Maybe you're even thinking of keeping a mallet beside the bed to knock yourself out. Thankfully, there are easier ways to sleep better—and to preach a better sermon in your sleep. Here are some ways you can improve your sleep habits.

Knowledge

If our schools substituted sleepology for algebra, our society would be much healthier, safer, and brighter. Despite sleep taking up a quarter to a third of our lives and having such an influence on the remainder, most of us leave school in total ignorance of the why and the how of sleep. As knowledge not only guides us but also motivates us, why not follow up some of the footnotes in this chapter or read *The Power of Rest* by sleep doctor Matthew Edlund (ignoring the new-agey bits) or *And So to Bed . . . : A Biblical View of Sleep* by Adrian Reynolds.[15]

Also, get to know yourself better and honestly work out how much sleep you really need to thrive. Most people need between seven and nine hours of sleep every day. I can do well

14. John Piper, "Charles Spurgeon: Preaching through Adversity," Desiring God, January 31, 1995, http://www.desiringgod.org/biographies/charles-spurgeon-preaching -through-adversity.

15. Adrian Reynolds, *And So to Bed . . . : A Biblical View of Sleep* (Fearn, Tain, Rossshire: Christian Focus, 2014); Matthew Edlund, *The Power of Rest: Why Sleep Alone Is Not Enough* (New York: Harper Collins, 2010).

on seven hours and even better on seven and a half hours, but eight or more hours doesn't seem to make any appreciable difference. If I get less than seven for a few days or more, consequences begin to multiply. Find your sweet spot and stick with it.

Discipline

Knowledge alone is not enough; we need planning, willpower, and discipline to make the necessary adjustments to our expectations, our schedules, and our lifestyles. We need to ask God to help us see this as a life priority, as a matter of obedience, and as a way of pleasing our Father and Creator. Let's plead with him to give us the strength to do what we know we must do.

Routine

If we strive for consistency in our bedtime, in our rising time, and in our pre-bed routine, our bodies will learn the routine, build a rhythm, and inject the right chemicals that prepare us for sleep. As Edlund writes:

> Preparing for sleep can be as important as what time you go to sleep. Your body is not built to dart suddenly from extreme mental and physical activity into immediate slumber. Rest and activity demand transitions. . . . Everything works better if much of your presleep period becomes routine, rhythmic, and ritualized. As you perform a sleep ritual night after night, your brain and body get used to the idea that this little group of behaviors will help you sleep and will provide you complete rest.[16]

---

16. Edlund, *The Power of Rest*, Kindle edition, locs. 959, 972.

Media Fast

A friend couldn't figure out why he was finding it difficult to sleep and was waking up frequently with bad dreams. Eventually he admitted he was watching movies just before trying to sleep! If we stimulate our brains (and body chemistry) with email, Facebook, films, TV news, computer games, *SportsCenter*, caffeine, or other energizers, we're asking for delayed and disturbed sleep—and we'll get it.

Family Cooperation

Noisy late-night teenagers or a wife who prefers to stay up late can make it difficult to establish earlier bedtimes and longer sleep times. A family conference may be necessary to explore ways to help one another make the compromises necessary to secure sufficient sleep for everybody. We have established a ten o'clock noise curfew for Sunday to Thursday nights. On Friday and Saturday, it's eleven o'clock.

Exercise

If we just sit at our desks or in our cars all day and then expect to be tired enough to sleep, we can expect some protests from our bodies: "Hey, you haven't done anything with me yet!" In an experiment at Loughborough University, it was found that exercising between three and six hours before sleep improved sleep.[17]

Contentment

Perhaps materialism and ambition are the biggest causes of sleep deprivation in our culture. People look at the idea of

---

17. Ibid., loc. 1174.

spending about a third of life asleep, thereby "losing" more than twenty years of their lives, and think, "I can make much more money and become much more successful (or build a bigger church), if I cut back on that." Most people who try this make some short-term gains but lose more in the long term, as their health is gradually impacted and their lives shortened. Contentment is a wonderful cure for insomnia.

Faith

Although short-term sleep medications may sometimes be required in extreme need, faith is one of the best (but least used) sleeping pills in the world—and it has only good side effects.

If I'm struggling to sleep, I use faith in God's Word to banish my anxiety. I pray: "Heavenly Father, I believe Matthew 6:25–27, which tells me you care for me more than the sparrows, and I can trust you to provide for me in every way. So I cast my cares upon you knowing that you care for me."

Faith helps me obey God's command to sleep: "Father, even though I think that sleeping less and working longer will benefit me and even your church, I believe Psalm 127:2, which says it is vain, it is utterly pointless, for me to rise too early or stay up too late."

Faith enables me to gladly receive sleep as a gift of God: "Father, although I sometimes see sleep as an intrusion, as a necessary evil, I believe Psalm 3:5, that sleep is your loving gift to me, and I take it gratefully."

Faith evaporates my fears: "Father, I'm sometimes afraid for my job, my church, or my country, but I believe Psalm 4:8, which says, 'I will both lie down in peace, and sleep; for you alone, O Lord, make me dwell in safety.'"

Counseling

One man asked me: "What about when griefs, fears, sorrows, and stresses are such that even when I am trying to sleep, sleep is elusive? And if these are accumulating, I can start feeling additional stress over the fact that I am not getting enough sleep."

When I'm in that vortex, I find it helpful to write down everything that's bothering me, together with the next step I will take to deal with each problem. Then, when anxiety raises its head as mine hits the pillow, I can point to the list and say, "I know about that and I have a plan to deal with it."

But in more serious cases of insomnia, counseling can play an important healing role. My friend Paul had been counseling himself through journaling and through reading a helpful book, *The Anxiety Cure* by Archibald Hart,[18] which he described as "a lifesaver." "But," he admitted, "I hadn't taken seriously the need to work on my unbiblical, sinful, and quite counterproductive habits of thought that contributed to my downturns." That's when Paul started getting biblical cognitive-behavioral counseling from a Christian pastor in the area. He went on:

> I was determined to get a rein on my mental world, regardless of what my body's chemistry was doing or not doing. It was the missing piece. It took time, but I have increasingly grown in my mastery over these spiritual, mental, and emotional toxins: mind-reading, excessive second-guessing, oversensitivity, putting too much stock in people's opinions of me, over-troubleshooting others' problems, and assuming the worst of people and situations. I began enjoying victory over my mind in bed. I was

---

18. Archibald Hart, *The Anxiety Cure* (Nashville: Thomas Nelson, 2001).

actually finding the mental switch—after too many years of assuming it was unfindable—to turn off thoughts that crept in on my pillow. "Sorry, thought. It is time for sleep now. Come back and visit me tomorrow. Nighty-night!"

Humility

By sleeping, we are relinquishing control and reminding our-selves—at least for a few hours—that God actually doesn't need us. When we close our eyes each night, we are saying, "I don't run the world, or the church, or even my own little life." Even the president has to get into his or her pajamas every night, effectively (if unwillingly) confessing that God doesn't need him or her, that there is a greater Superpower. But the Christian's sleep should be different from the non-Christian's. When and how long we sleep makes a huge state-ment about who we are and what we believe about ourselves and God.

Men can find it especially hard to admit their need for increased sleep, especially if they have survived for many years on less. That's where an objective outside voice can help us humble ourselves and accept our limitations. A burnt-out Christian man admitted to me: "Sleep has been vital in my 'reset.' And it's almost like I needed permission from my counselor to convince myself that I was not getting enough sleep, and that I needed to take a couple weeks off to recal-ibrate."

One pastor confessed that he had been depriving himself of sleep for years because "that's what the Puritans did." If they could do it, why couldn't he? After eventually accepting that his frail humanity needed rest, he said:

Everyone's schedule is different, and sleep needs vary. As long as we are working hard while we work and getting the sleep our body needs, we are honoring the Lord. In fact, I was quite dishonoring God by saying, "I realize you tell me in Psalm 127 that sleep is a gift. But really, why don't you give it to somebody else? Somebody more needy. Somebody less superhuman. Some mere mortal, on whom the world is not depending so much?" I was also abusing coffee, trying to compensate. I was a paper Calvinist, but a closet Pelagian, working more by law than by love. Work is good. But it's only good if it's anchored and totally conditioned by grace. Now I'm receiving grace and receiving the grace of sleep. Because my Father is good and I am needy.

Acceptance of Special Periods

There are times when things don't work out, when sleep is delayed or shortened for one reason or another. For example, we may have to go with less sleep during special seasons of extra work or ministry. We should not be too worried about brief periods of such intensity. God can sustain us through such exceptional times. But if that becomes our pattern and habit, we won't be working or ministering well or for long.

People often point to famous Christians "who only slept one hour a week" (I exaggerate—slightly). What is not said is that many of them then suffered horrendous ill health and not a few died quite young. We have only a limited amount of fuel in our tanks, and that fuel will run out eventually. If we drive at 90 mph with hardly a rest break, that fuel is going to run out much quicker than for those who take their mortality seriously, look after their engines, and drive economically.

Napping

I drink too much coffee to make this work for me, but many have found that a fifteen- to twenty-minute daytime nap improves productivity, moods, and interpersonal relationships, so much so that some high-tech companies have set up "nap-pods" or "napping areas" for staff members. One NASA study found that naps averaging twenty-six minutes improved work performance on some tasks by 38 percent.[19] Another study of top violinists found that as well as sleeping for 8.6 hours a night, an hour longer than the average American, they also spent almost three hours a week napping.[20]

Even if you don't always sleep, the relaxation of a nap time can be incredibly refreshing. As one man explained to me: "My evening 'power snooze' on the couch after supper gives me a boost of energy. I don't really sleep, but consciously relax for fifteen to twenty minutes. Others can make all the noise they want; it doesn't bother me at all. I remember my dad doing the same thing when we were small."

Sleep Doctor

But what if you've tried all these things and you're still exhausted through lack of sleep? It's not that you're neglecting sleep. No, you desperately want to sleep but can't. Perhaps the problem may have a physical component, maybe something like sleep apnea, in which case, visiting a specialist sleep

---

19. Cited in Edlund, *The Power of Rest*, loc. 1666.
20. K. Anders Ericcson et al., "The Role of Deliberate Practice in the Acquisition of Expert Performance," *Psychological Review 1993*, Vol. 100. No. 3, 363–406.

doctor may be part of the solution. According to the Centers for Disease Control and Prevention, "about fifty- to seventy-million U.S. adults have sleep or wakefulness disorder."[21]

Sleep Theology

Ultimately, sleep, like everything else, should lead us to the gospel and the Savior. First, it prompts us to think about *death*, that we all shall close our eyes as in sleep, and wake up in another world (1 Thess. 4:14).

It also teaches about our *Savior*. The fact that Jesus slept (Mark 4:38) is as profound as "Jesus wept" (John 11:35). It reminds us of Christ's full humanity, that the Son of God became so frail, so weak, so human that he needed to sleep. What humility! What love! What an example! What a comfort! What a sleeping pill!

It illustrates *salvation*. How much are we doing when we sleep? Nothing! That's why Jesus used rest as an illustration of his salvation. "Come to me, all you who labor and are heavy laden, and I will give you rest" (Matt. 11:28).

It points us toward *heaven*. There remains a rest for the people of God (Heb. 4:9). That doesn't mean heaven is going to be one long lie-in. It means it will be a place of renewal, refreshment, comfort, and perfect peace.

I hope this repair bay helps you sleep more soundly—and have a sounder theology! But now I want you to wake up, roll into the fourth repair bay, and get your gym kit on as we work out in the repair bay of "Re-Create."

---

21. "Insufficient Sleep Is a Public Health Problem," Centers for Disease Control and Prevention, September 3, 2015, http://www.cdc.gov/features/dssleep/.

Re-Create

C

It was fall 2006, and President Bush's "Mission Accomplished" was turning into "Mission Impossible" as the United States was slowly yet surely losing the Iraq War. General George Casey was persisting in the bloody "drawdown to handover" strategy, despite the engulfing disaster. Marine General Peter Pace, chairman of the Joint Chiefs of Staff, was desperate. Looking for a new strategy, he invited retired Army General Jack Keane to a crisis meeting and asked for his honest feedback.[1]

Keane was blisteringly frank and direct: "I would give you a failing grade."

Visibly pained, Pace asked, "What do you think I should be doing?"

Keane's advice was startling: Pace should tell General Casey to reduce his workload and take time off every day. He went on: "George Casey is at this 24/7. He has nothing

---

1. Bob Woodward reports the encounter in *The War Within: A Secret White House History 2006–2008* (New York: Simon & Schuster, 2008), 144ff.

to nurture his life. He is completely immersed and isolated by one thing and only one thing. That's this war. It has completely captured everything he does. His capacity at times to see clearly is always going to be limited and defined by his day-in, day-out experience and the fatigue he suffers."

Keane then addressed what he saw as the obsessive work ethic of the senior American military commanders. "Our generals fight wars today almost at a frenetic pace that is counterproductive," he said. Journalist Bob Woodward writes:

> [Keane suggested that Pace compare the current U.S. generals] to World War II General Douglas MacArthur, who watched a movie every night, or Army Chief of Staff George Marshall, who went home every night at a reasonable hour and "rode a horse, for crying out loud, and sometimes took a nap for an hour and a half during the day. And these guys were doing big, important things. You know what our guys are like? They're at their desks at 6:30 in the morning, and they stay up till midnight."
>
> It was a manhood issue, Keane thought. Because the soldiers were out there 24/7, the generals thought they better do the same. But the core issue was fresh, clear thinking about the tasks of war.

Keene's point was that "fresh, clear thinking" was possible only if the generals had time away from the desk, time to nurture their lives, time for recreation.

Many of us men need a General Keane in our lives. It is so easy for us to be doing, doing, doing; producing, producing, producing; more, more, more; longer, longer, longer. Yet are we losing battle after battle, and maybe even the war? Is our obsessive work ethic self-defeating? In trying to impress other men with our manly work rate (and pastors are especially susceptible to this), are we destroying our ability to think about our callings, our problems, and our challenges in fresh, clear ways?

Although we can certainly find better recreation than watching movies every night, and safer things to do than riding horses in our cities, the principle is the same: we must nurture our lives with regular recreation, especially physical exercise. Maybe, just maybe, a bit less work and a bit more play could turn our present "Mission Impossible" into "Mission Accomplished!"

In Repair Bay 2, we spent some time exploring what it means to be a creature and how we can "uncreate" ourselves by ignoring our creatureliness, leading to disrepair and disintegration in various areas of our lives. In Repair Bay 3, we explored rest as one of the ways God has provided for us to renew and reset our lives. Repair Bay 4 introduces a second way, re-creation by recreation, especially by the grace of bodily exercise.

But before we get to the more practical section, let's lay the foundation of a gospel-centered theology of the body. We need this background because the way to begin and sustain regular physical exercise is not so much by monastic self-discipline or by the insane enthusiasm of some fitness instructors, but by grasping the inspiring and motivational truths of the gospel. Let's look at some of these powerful truths.

Body Theology

As evidenced by the vast amount of money spent on health care, cosmetics, and plastic surgery, the majority of people are obsessed with their bodies. In contrast, the church of Christ has rightly emphasized the soul. What's the point in having a healthy and beautiful body if the soul is sick and ugly (Mark 8:36)? The body will eventually deteriorate, weaken, sicken, and die. But the soul can get stronger and healthier with the passing of years (Ps. 92:12–15; 2 Cor. 4:16).

The church, however, has often emphasized the soul to the exclusion of, or the minimizing of, the body. As a result, neglecting the body is sometimes seen as a virtue or a mark of superspirituality. One pastor explained his struggle with this to me:

> Somewhere along the way I equated recreation with worldliness. If it wasn't directly advancing the Kingdom I didn't need to be doing it. I secretly thought that God would look down and see that I was taking ministry so seriously that he would bless me. But I wasn't living like a human being. I didn't realize how much I needed these things. I needed to experience beauty and creativity. I needed to enjoy God's gifts without guilt. It was a matter of survival.

He's right. And such errors can be defeated only with truth, with the Bible's theology of the body. Yes, the Bible does have a theology of the body, much of it contained in 1 Corinthians 6:9–20:

Your body is damaged by sin (vv. 9–10). Though sin begins in our souls, we sin in and with our bodies. That's why Paul begins his *Body Theology* by confessing the sin that damages and even destroys our bodies.

Your body is saved by God (v. 11). "And such *were* some of you" (past tense). You were *that*—but you are now *this*. You were defiled, damaged, destroyed, but now you are washed, sanctified, justified. Yes, we can take our dirty, damaged, dying bodies and souls to God, and he sets his Son and Spirit to work on them. This is a full-body and full-soul salvation.

Your body remains vulnerable (v. 12). Although he knows he has experienced a body-and-soul salvation, the apostle is conscious of his remaining spiritual and physical weakness and vulnerability. Many things are permissible, but he doesn't want to hinder his re-creation by doing what is not beneficial or helpful. He is not free from the need for daily discipline of his bodily appetites.

Your body is for the Lord (vv. 13–14). The apostle replaces a false slogan the Corinthians were using to abuse their bodies—"foods for the stomach and the stomach for foods"—with a true slogan to bless their bodies: "The body is . . . for the Lord, and the Lord for the body."

"The body is for the Lord." God has given each of us a body to give back to him. He did not give us a body so that we can give it to anybody and everybody in immoral sexual relations. He did not give us a body so that we can give it to overwork or sloth. He gave us a body to give back to him. The body is for the Lord.

"The Lord is for the body." He made it, cares for it, and maintains an eternal interest in it. He even took on a body, suffered in a body, and rose again in a body. He has a body to this day. The Lord is for the body. This is not of minor importance. Our future resurrection shows how much honor God puts on the body and how much we should honor in the meantime what he will honor for all time.

Your body is a member of Christ (vv. 15–17). Yes, our souls are members of Christ's body. But so are our bodies! And that has huge implications for how we view and treat them. When my father was a dentist, he told me that by looking at a person's teeth, he could tell how much money that person earned and whether he was in good overall health! One little part of the body revealed so much about the whole person. Paul is using this reality to motivate all members of Christ's body to view and treat their bodies as revealing something positive or negative about Christ.

Your body is a temple of the Holy Spirit (vv. 18–19). Home Depot, Lowe's, and Menards are always busy, thanks to people repairing, upgrading, and beautifying their homes. No one is buying tools and equipment to damage or destroy their homes. And yet, are we damaging or even destroying the Holy Spirit's home by our overactivity or inactivity!

Your body was bought with a price (v. 20). How would you respond if I said to you: "Could you take a bit more care of my back please? You're not sitting very well in your chair, and I don't want my back to suffer a herniated or prolapsed disc!" Or what would you say if I interrupted your ice cream with: "Do you think you could eat a bit less sugar and a bit more whole wheat? It's really much better for my stomach."

You might well respond: "Who do you think you are?" "What right do you have to tell me what to do with my body?" or "What do you mean by *your* back or *your* stomach? They're mine, not yours."

I then answer: "Actually, you are not your own. You don't own your body. I'm your body's owner. I bought your body a few weeks back, and I'm just taking care of what's mine."

That's really what God is saying here through Paul: "You are not your own, for you were bought with a price. Therefore, please take much more care of *my* body." And the more we calculate the price paid for our bodies by the precious blood of Christ, the more we sense an obligation to our new owner. We've been bought with a price. We are not our own.

Therefore, glorify God in your body and in your spirit, which are God's (v. 20). Paul's argument is: God created us body and soul and redeemed us body and soul, so we are to serve him body and soul. Our souls and bodies are his and for his glory. That should make a difference in how we view them and treat them.

If that's a theology of the body, what does it mean in terms of practice? How do we glorify God with our bodies? For those of us who need a life reset, we can put this body theology into practice with three physical actions that will help re-create our bodies as we live out grace-paced lives: standing up, exercising, and doing manual work.

Stand Up

"Men who spend more than twenty-three hours per week sitting have a 64 percent greater chance of dying from heart disease than those who sit for eleven hours a week or less."[2] That's not good news for the ever-increasing majority of us who spend most of our time behind desks or steering wheels. Numerous studies have shown that we are sitting down more than ever before in history (an average of 9.3 hours a day), and such sustained periods of sitting do really bad things to our bodies, including increasing our risk of heart disease, obesity, diabetes, and certain cancers.[3] Sitting six-plus hours per

2. Gretchen Reynolds, "Phys Ed: The Men Who Stare at Screens," *The New York Times*, July 14, 2010, http://well.blogs.nytimes.com/2010/07/14/phys-ed-the-men-who-stare-at-screens/.

3. Peter T. Katzmarzyk et al., "Sitting Time and Mortality from All Causes, Cardiovascular Disease, and Cancer," *Medicine and Science in Sports and Exercise* 41,

day makes us up to 40 percent likelier to die within fifteen years than someone who sits less than three. Thanks to Bill Gates and Steve Jobs, as our productivity has increased, so has our mortality. What a contrast with the past, when the vast majority of the population did manual work. Now, the most exercised parts of our bodies are our fingertips.

If you are a desk-dweller, part of the solution might be a stand-up desk that would enable you to stand at least from time to time throughout the day. Though some of these are expensive, there are a number of possibilities for under $200. I started with a $50 do-it-yourself version made with materials from Lowe's and recently graduated to one that I can raise or lower at the push of a button. Now, instead of sitting down for an average of eight hours a day, I alternate between one hour of sitting and one hour of standing. It's made a huge difference to my energy and concentration levels, and hopefully also my longevity.

Exercise

Moderate physical exercise helps to expel unhelpful chemicals from our systems and stimulates the production of helpful chemicals. It strengthens not just the body but also the brain. Research has shown that walking just two miles a day reduces the risk of cognitive decline and dementia by 60 percent. And aside from the long-term benefits, exercise triggers the growth of new brain cells in the hippocampus and the

no. 5 (May 2009): 998–1005, http://journals.lww.com/acsm-msse/Fulltext/2009/05000 /Sitting_Time_and_Mortality_from_All_Causes,.5.aspx; Olivia Judson, "Stand Up While You Read This," *The New York Times*, February 23, 2010, http://opinionator.blogs.ny times.com/2010/02/23/stand-up-while-you-read-this/?_r=0; Neville Owen et al., "Too Much Sitting: The Population Health Science of Sedentary Behavior," *Exercise Sports Science Review* 38, no. 3 (July 2010): 105–113, http://www.ncbi.nlm.nih.gov/pubmed /20577058.

release of neurotrophic growth factors—a kind of mental fertilizer that helps the brain grow, maintain new connections, and stay healthy.[4] Exercise and proper rest patterns generate about a 20 percent energy increase in an average day,[5] while exercising three to five times a week is about as effective as antidepressants for mild to moderate depression.[6]

Ken underlined this in a letter to me: "I cannot overemphasize the effect exercise has on my mood. It is clearly one of those activities that demonstrate the connection between mind and body. When I was in my deepest depression, exercise kept me from going over the edge. When I recovered, it kept me from sliding back in."

In September 2014, aged forty-eight, I finally admitted that I needed to add exercise into my life. I talked to one of my students who was a part-time trainer at the YMCA. I wanted to start pumping iron (and building my biceps), but he persuaded me to start with his group fitness class that would condition my whole body. A few days later, when I opened the gym door for the "Bodypump" class, I was confronted with twenty to thirty women in various shapes and shades of Lycra. I was about to say, "Sorry, wrong room," and run for

---

4. Norman Doidge, "Our Amazingly Plastic Brains," *The Wall Street Journal*, February 6, 2015, http://www.wsj.com/articles/our-amazingly-plastic-brains-1423262095. See also Madhumita Murgia, "How Stress Affects Your Brain," *TedEd*, February 20, 2015, http://ed.ted.com/lessons/how-stress-affects-your-brain-madhumita-murgia; Nicole Spartano et al., "Midlife Exercise Blood Pressure, Heart Rate, and Fitness Relate to Brain Volume 2 Decades Later," *Neurology*, February 10, 2016, http://www.neurology.org/content/early/2016/02/10/WNL.0000000000002415.

5. Sam Fahmy, "Low-Intensity Exercise Reduces Fatigue Symptoms by 65 Percent, Study Finds," *UGA Today*, February 28, 2008, http://news.uga.edu/releases/article/low-intensity-exercise-reduces-fatigue-symptoms-by-65-percent-study-finds.

6. M. Babyak et al., "Exercise Treatment for Major Depression: Maintenance of Therapeutic Benefit at 10 Months," *Journal of Psychosomatic Medicine* 62, no. 5 (September-October 2000): 633–38, http://www.ncbi.nlm.nih.gov/pubmed/11020092; Andrea L. Dunn et al., "Exercise Treatment for Depression: Efficacy and Dose Response," *American Journal of Preventive Medicine* 28, no. 1 (January 2005): 1–8, http://www.ajpmonline.org/article/S0749-3797(04)00241-7/abstract.

my life when my student saw me and called me in. I smiled weakly as he squeezed me into a small space at the front of the class with a mat, a step, and a few weights. Within five minutes, I was a gibbering wreck of jelly, my arms aching and my legs collapsing. Meanwhile, all the women were outlifting and outstepping me in every exercise. It was utterly humiliating, and I made a mental note to fail the student at the next exam. He later assured me that there were usually a couple of men there and that I had to return. I did, but I made sure to take Shona with me to make it clear that I was not some sad, desperate, middle-aged male looking for a younger woman. The bonus was that it got my wife started as well.

Before long, I'd left the Lycra ladies behind. I now pump iron four days a week following a personalized training program. I sometimes wish I could go back to the class just to show the women the man of steel I have become. But I resist it.

So I've learned quite a bit about starting a fitness regimen, with these being the main lessons:

Get Advice

If you are really out of shape, you should see your doctor before beginning any kind of exercise program. If he gives you the all clear, then why not join a local gym or YMCA, where you can either get a few sessions with a personal trainer or join one of the group classes? Either way, you'll have the confidence that you are doing the right thing in the right way.

Have a Clear Aim

Motivation is the key to exercise. What's your "Why?" Is it to lose weight? Is it to build strength or stamina? What's your aim and how will you know if you are reaching it? If you can get clarity on these questions, you've won half the battle. My initial aim was to lose about fifteen pounds of weight and then begin to build lean muscle. The first part was easy to see on the scales and in the mirror; sadly, the second isn't so easy to see in the mirror (yet), but I certainly feel a lot stronger and I don't suffer back pain so regularly. I also log my daily targets on a spreadsheet app on my phone so that I can be encouraged by progress.

Build Slowly

It's tempting, especially for type A high achievers, to start off a drive for physical fitness by running a marathon or bench-pressing two-hundred pounds. If you aim too high, you'll fail. You will either injure yourself, discourage yourself, or embarrass yourself.

If you're really out of shape, begin with a twenty-minute walk each day, then lengthen it, then speed it up, and then move slowly toward jogging. Even walking increases blood flow, improves your waste management, renews cells, and lowers blood pressure and stress.

Or start with light weights, see how your body responds, and gradually increase. Even now, months down the line, I'm still learning the importance of stressing the muscles enough to increase strength and stamina, but not so much that I rip or damage them, leaving me kicking my heels on the sidelines for days or even weeks as I wait for healing.

Have a Weekly Routine

Because of the power of habit, it's easier to do something regularly and routinely rather than just when we feel like it or just when we can fit it in. My fixed weekly gym routine is four thirty to five thirty on Monday, Tuesday, Thursday, and Friday afternoons. It's now so much part of my life that I hardly need to think about it. I no longer have a daily internal argument: "Will I or won't I?" It's like breathing; I don't have to make a decision about it; it just kind of happens. My body now expects its workout and even misses it if I have to skip a day.

Mix It Up

Exercising at the same time each day does not mean doing the same exercise every day. We need to exercise all the different parts of the body, varying the workout so that we don't get bored and our bodies don't get used to the same exercises and end up plateauing. I alternate weights with cardio, I work out different parts each day, and I mix in some stretching as well.

Play

It's so important to enjoy physical exercise. If we are just grinding out the miles, reps, and sets, exercising will just become another round of performance targets as it morphs from a grace to be received into a law to be obeyed. All the pleasure and benefit will drain away, and eventually we will give it up. If this is a temptation for you, then look for an activity, exercise, game, or sport that you can enjoy doing so it won't be an additional source of stress. As Roald Dahl once said, "A little nonsense now and then, is cherished by the wisest men."[7] If we can do this outdoors, all the better, due to the therapeutic impact of sunshine and fresh air.

---

7. Roald Dahl, *Charlie and the Chocolate Factory* (New York: Puffin, 1998), 88.

Be Accountable

Keeping a record of your daily exercise can also form the basis of accountability with your trainer or with a friend or your wife. I know that if I come home from work and I'm still in my shirt and tie, my wife will say, "Oh, you didn't go to the gym today?" The next day she'll say, "You didn't go the gym again!" Day three never happens.

Manual Work

Sometimes I am envious of house painters, plumbers, landscapers, carpenters, and others who get to work with their hands and have something to show for it at the end of every day, or at least every week. What do I and other "knowledge workers" have to show for our work every seven days?

Virtually nothing.

This is because most of it actually *is* "virtual"—words that are hidden inside our computers and servers in files, documents, reports, spreadsheets, and so on. There's not a lot of physicality to this. In my case, some of the words become sermons or lectures, which also seem to largely evaporate into the air as they are spoken. For knowledge workers in general, and for pastors in particular, there often just isn't anything to show for weeks and weeks, months and months, years and years of mental sweat, blood, and tears. Pastor Jim explains the pain of this discouragement:

> In ten years of ministry, I have worked very hard with little to show for it. I spent several hours every week doing outreach. I thought I was able to convince myself, God is sovereign, and the results are in his hands. He will give rain when he wants. William Carey worked for all those

years with precious little fruit. But deep down, it was beginning to rattle me.

As Jim said, one answer to this frustrating sense of futility is more faith to believe that God will bless his Word written and spoken. We sow the seed, another waters, but God gives the increase. Yes, we believe all that—most of the time. But we're still human; we still have a basic human need to see some fruit, some result, something to show for all the hours and hours in the study and on our knees.

Another answer is a hobby or pastime that meets this basic human need to have something physical or visible at the end of it, something to point to, something beautiful to see and admire. For me, it might be something as simple as a freshly mown lawn, a painted room, or a king salmon. For you, it could be a painting, a piece of woodwork, a vegetable garden, or a lower golf score. It's anything physical that is produced by enjoyable physical activity, done every week if possible.[8]

A friend of mine laughs at men who go to the gym every week and then get a riding mower or pay someone to plow their snow. As he said: "Sweating is good for a man, but sweating while mowing or plowing is much better then just sweating at the gym. You are doing something productive while you are getting your body in better shape." A pastor told me: "I am so grateful that God has given me woodworking as a creative outlet. I call it my therapy. I especially like making gifts for family members because I will usually see them again. When I do, it brings great satisfaction. This might seem silly but pastors need something they can see."

---

8. See Tim Challies, "Hobbies to the Glory of God," *Challies.com*, March 9, 2016, http://www.challies.com/articles/hobbies-to-the-glory-of-god.

On top of that weekly infusion of satisfaction, I also try to do one major physical project every year. One year, I laid a patio. Last year, I built a deck in our yard. This year, I bought a chainsaw to tidy up the forest behind my home and cut up some fallen trees. Again, this is something tangible I can point to and say, "I did that!" (with God's help, of course). Maybe, at least sometimes, the apostle Paul got a greater sense of accomplishment from gluing and stitching tents together than gluing and stitching ripped churches together.

Yes, I also pray for more faith that God will bless my ministry. But like many knowledge workers, there's still a little bit of me—maybe it's a really weak and carnal bit—that just needs the regular encouragement of something I can see and touch. Grass, paving stone, and wood have worked for me. The dirtier and harder the work, the better.

It's not just pastors who have this craving. One friend, a business consultant, mourned: "All the creation that I do in my daily work is intangible. . . . What I dislike about my work is that it's all done in meetings, on the phone, and on the computer. My kids don't get to see me 'working' in anything that looks like work to their minds." He also has turned to manual work because "it gives me a great sense of accomplishment. I can SEE what I accomplished in those hours. I can touch and feel and even show others what I did with my hands. It's tangible." He also tries to involve his kids and even his friends in his projects, saying, "Manual labor is the place where I get to work, exercise, breathe fresh air, create something tangible, and do all of that in the company of family and friends. As my kids have grown, my commitment to manual labor and DIY projects has increased."

Strangely, rather than become a substitute for my knowledge work in the study, physical work in the yard has also motivated, inspired, and energized me to do more spiritual work too. Likewise, one pastor who had to use an antidepressant for a short time told me, "Exercising has certainly been more powerful and effective than the antidepressant; it replenishes me, clarifies my thinking, and helps me maintain physical fitness and sustain happiness." He called exercise "strategic disengagement in order to nurture our souls and our bodies." Although it sounds counterintuitive, exercise science confirms that daily exercise and proper rest patterns boost energy by about 20 percent a day. That's how your "Mission Impossible" can become "Mission Accomplished."

But now, after all that exercise and manual work, you'll be glad to know that we're going to relax. Yes, we need to get our bodies moving again, but we also need to learn how and when to unwind, both physically and mentally. Living a grace-paced life receives the grace of sweating, but also the grace of chilling.

Relax

Ↄ

How about this for a book title: *10% Happier: How I Tamed the Voice in My Head, Reduced Stress without Losing My Edge, and Found Self-Help That Actually Works—A True Story*. In it, *Good Morning America* presenter Dan Harris describes his sincere but often bizarre search for happiness, which took him to many weird and wonderful people, places, and practices until he settled on a fairly extreme form of yoga-related meditation that made him, oh, about 10 percent happier.

At the end of it, you think, "Wow, all that effort to be just 10 percent happier!" Yet Harris still thinks it was worth it, especially for learning the ability to live only in the present, a practice often called "mindfulness." The idea is to get to a state of mind that does not think backward or forward, that doesn't remember the past or anticipate the future. With the assistance of a breathing technique, the mind is emptied of everything but the present moment. Perfectly focused on only the here and now, the practitioner of this technique enjoys a state of mental bliss. If you think that's easy to achieve, read the book, or, better, try it yourself. As Harris concedes, it's like cage fighting with a fish:

> It was a rigorous brain exercise: rep after rep of trying to tame the runaway train of the mind. The repeated attempt to bring the compulsive thought machine to heel was like holding a live fish in your hands. Wrestling your mind to the ground, repeatedly hauling your attention back to the breath in the face of the inner onslaught required genuine grit.[1]

While it's both sad and funny to read about Harris's harrowing and often humorous journey, there's something about this book title that contains a nugget of truth: one of the keys to a happier and less stressful life is turning down the volume dial in our minds and enjoying internal calm and quiet. The grace of peace is a vital part of a grace-paced life. We need rest for the body *and* the mind. As the psalmist said, "Be still, and know that I am God" (Ps. 46:10).

Our Inner Orchestra

Every Christian wants to know God more; few Christians sequester the silence that this requires. Instead, we spend our days smashing stillness-shattering, knowledge-destroying cymbals on our ears and in our souls.

With so many gongs and clashes in our lives, it can sometimes be difficult to isolate and identify them. So let me help you do this and then provide some mufflers.[2]

---

1. Dan Harris, *10% Happier: How I Tamed the Voice in My Head, Reduced Stress without Losing My Edge, and Found Self-Help That Actually Works—A True Story* (New York: HarperCollins, 2014), Kindle edition, loc. 101.

2. Part of this section was previously published in "Silencing the Cymbals," *Tabletalk* magazine, June 2012. Used with permission.

First, there's the din of guilt, the shame and embarrassment of our dark moral secrets: thoughts of "I should have . . . I shouldn't have . . . I should have . . . I shouldn't have . . ." clang noisily in our deep recesses, shattering our peace and disturbing our tranquility.

Then greed starts banging away in our hearts with its relentless drumstick: "I want it . . . I need it . . . I must have it . . . I will have it . . . I got it . . . I want it . . . I need it . . ." and so on.

And what's that angry metal beat? It's hate stirring up malice, ill will, resentment, and revenge: "How could she . . . ? I'll get him . . . She'll pay for this." Of course, anger often clatters into the cymbal of controversy, sparking disagreements, debates, disputes, and divisions.

Vanity also adds its proud and haughty thud, drowning out all who compete with our beauty, our talents, and our status: "Me up, him down. Me up, her down. Me up, all down."

Anxiety tinkles distractingly in the background too, rapidly surveying the past, the present, and the future for things to worry about: "What if . . . ? What if . . . ? What if . . . ?" And is that the little silver triangle of self-pity I hear: "Why me? Why me? Why me?"

The repetitive and unstoppable jangle of expectation comes from all directions—family members, friends, employers, church, and, especially, ourselves. Oh, for even a few seconds of respite from the tyranny of other people's demands and especially from our demanding, oversensitive consciences.

And smashing into our lives wherever we turn are the giant cymbals of the media and technology: local and international, paper and pixels, sound and image, audio and video, beep and tweet, notifications and reminders, and on and on it goes.

Is it any wonder that we sometimes feel as if we're going mad? We live amid constant clanking and clanging, jingling and jangling, smashing and crashing, grating and grinding—a large, jarring orchestra of peace-disturbing, soul-dismantling cymbals.

Then we read, "Be still and know that I am God."

But how?

Silencing the Cymbals

We can silence the cymbal of guilt by taking faith to the blood of Christ and saying, "Believe!" You must believe that all your sins are paid for and pardoned. There's absolutely no reason to have even one whisper of guilt. Look at that blood until you grasp how precious and how effective it is. It can make you whiter than snow and make your conscience quieter than the morning dew.

Greed is not easily silenced. Maybe muffled is about the best we can expect. Practice doing with less than usual, not buying even when you can afford it, buying nothing but necessities for a time, and spending time in the shadow of Calvary. How much less you'll find you need when you see how much Christ gave! Draw up your budget at the cross (2 Cor. 8:9).

Our unholy anger can be dialed down by God's holy anger. When we feel God's hot rage against all sin and all injustice, we begin to chill and calm. Vengeance is God's; he will repay (Rom. 12:19).

The doctrine of total depravity is the ultimate dampener of personal vanity. When I see myself as God sees me, my heart, my mind, and even my posture change. I stop competing for the top spot and start accepting the lowest place. "He must increase, but I must decrease" (John 3:30).

Hey! I'm beginning to hear some quiet now. But there's still that rankling anxiety tinkling away. Oh, to be free of that!

Fatherhood.

What?

Yes, the fatherhood of God can turn the volume of anxiety to zero. He knows, he cares, and he will provide for your needs. Mute your "What-ifs" at the bird feeder (Matt. 6:25–34).

Oh, and call in total depravity again when self-pity starts up. "Why me?" cannot stand long before "Why not me?"

"She has done what she could" (Mark 14:8). Don't you just love Christ's words to Mary when she anointed his head? What an expectation killer! Every time the despotic Devil, other people, or your tyrannical conscience demands more than you can give, remind them of Jesus's calming words: "She has done what she could."

Isn't that growing silence silver? But it can become golden if you go the extra mile and deal with the noisy intruders of media and technology. That's where I want us to focus for the next few pages. I want to help you build some speed bumps in your life, to slow you down and to quiet your heart and mind.

Daily Bumps

First, we'll construct some small *daily* bumps, then we'll raise a bigger *weekly* bump, and finally we'll conclude by raising some *quarterly*, *annual*, and *seasonal* bumps.

The Digital Deluge

Research indicates that Americans are consuming an average of fifteen and a half hours of traditional and digital media each day. That's seventy-four gigabytes a day uploaded to our minds![3] The report goes on to say, "While in the past media consumption was overwhelmingly passive—we sat and watched TV or listened to radio—new media consumption is increasingly interactive, with time-delayed, multi-tasking and interrupted viewership fast becoming the typical consumptive behavior."[4]

So the problem is not just information overload; it's also information bombardment. Men talk to me about their mental and emotional exhaustion, and all through the conversations, their phones are lighting up with a distracting blizzard of sounds and images. And they wonder why their brains feel fried! They're giving themselves continual mental whiplash as they pour stimuli and data into their brains from every direction.

Imagine that you went into the gym and saw a guy furiously working out his right bicep by spending about three seconds on one machine, then running over and doing three seconds on another, jumping from one exercise to another, pulling the muscle then pushing the muscle, using small weights with high reps and then big weights with low reps—all day long. That poor bicep wouldn't know what was coming next and just might say, "Enough, I'm done."

But that's how many of us are treating our brains. We wake, check email, turn on the TV, listen to the radio, sit down at the computer, answer the phone, respond to a text, open Facebook, comment on a blog, send a text, engage in conversation, write a report, counsel someone, plan for a meeting—and that's all before breakfast. Every single one

---

3. James E. Short, "How Much Media? 2015: Report on American Consumers," USC Marshall School of Business, https://www.marshall.usc.edu/faculty/centers/ctm/research/how-much-media.

4. Ibid.

of these activities makes demands on and drains our mind muscles, and the situation is especially damaging because we are jumping so rapidly from one mental exercise to another, giving the muscle no chance to recover or to build any rhythm. (And you thought the gym rat was mad!)

Want to restore some sanity? Here are five bumps that I've built (and keep having to rebuild) to protect and strengthen my brain.

I mute my phone and computer notifications. During my peak mental working hours, when I do most of my thinking, research, and writing (usually seven thirty in the morning to one in the afternoon), I mute my phone and turn off all email, text, and social media notifications. The longer I go uninterrupted, the calmer my mind, the better my focus, the deeper my thinking, and the more efficient my time management. And it's not just that I will not be interrupted; it's that I *know* I will not be interrupted. That produces a totally different mindset and mind depth than the one that's sub-consciously waiting for the next beep or ding. As Pablo Picasso is reputed to have said, "Without great solitude no serious work is possible."

Working without distractions and interruptions enables me to accomplish twice as much in half the time, allowing me more time to relax with my family. It also breaks the addiction element. Scientists have discovered that every time an email arrives or we get a retweet or a Facebook "like," our brains eject tiny squirts of pleasure chemical (it's like a mini crack cocaine hit). So every buzz or beep notification creates a craving in our bodies for the squirt-hit, turning us into beep- and pingaholics.

I check my email, phone, text messages, and social media four to six times a day. The average for "knowledge workers" is six times an hour! When I check in, I'm skimming for any "emergencies" or "urgents" that need immediate action, but these are rare. Most of the time, I delay responses until the late afternoon, when I try to process all communications in a thirty- to forty-five-minute window. Limiting the window forces me to limit the time I spend on each communication. I prioritize replies so that I do the most important first and make sure that any unanswered emails can wait until the next day.

I put my phone on my wife's desk when I get home. I don't carry my phone around the house with me or take it into the yard when I'm playing with the kids. Putting it in a place that I have to make an effort to get to reduces the likelihood of me checking in. It also increases the quality of my conversations. Massachusetts Institute of Technology Professor Sherry Turkle's "studies of conversation both in the laboratory and in natural settings show that when two people are talking, the mere presence of a phone on a table between them or in the periphery of their vision changes both what they talk about and the degree of connection they feel. . . . Even a silent phone disconnects us."[5]

I charge my phone in the kitchen overnight. I stopped using my phone as my alarm clock because having it beside my bed meant that I usually checked email and such last thing at night—which often made it difficult for me to sleep—and sometimes first thing in the morning, starting my mind whirring in every direction before I even had a chance to read my Bible and pray.

I fast from media. I do this in two ways. I don't email, blog,

---

5. Sherry Turkle, "Stop Googling. Let's Talk," *The New York Times*, September 26, 2015, http://www.nytimes.com/2015/09/27/opinion/sunday/stop-googling-lets-talk.html.

or read social media on vacations, and I usually avoid news media, blogs, and social media on Sundays.

Denver Seminary Professor Douglas Groothuis requires that his students abstain from an electronic medium for one week. He says:

> The results have been nothing less than profound for the vast majority of the students. Having withdrawn from the world of TV, radio, computers, they find more silence, time for reflection and prayer, and more opportunities to engage family and friends thoughtfully. They become more peaceful and contemplative—and begin to notice how media-saturated most of our culture has become.[6]

I'm sure you can think of other ways of calming the traffic in your mind—not checking the phone every time you are in a line or at a traffic light, taking walks without your phone, and so on—but these are the areas I'm working on, and when I succeed, I not only feel better, I am much more creative and productive. I've also come to realize that digital technology is one of the greatest impediments to a life spent in communion with God. To paraphrase Blaise Pascal, "All our miseries derive from not being able to sit in a quiet room alone [with God]."[7] We'd like it to be different. But as Psalm 46 confirms, God has inseparably and irrevocably joined quietness with knowledge of him. What God has joined together, let not man put asunder.

---

6. Douglas Groothuis, "Habits of the High Tech Heart: Living Virtuously in the Information Age," Denver Seminary, January 1, 2003, http://www.denverseminary .edu/resources/news-and-articles/habits-of-the-high-tech-heart-living-virtuously-in-the -information-age/.

7. For the original quotation, see Blaise Pascal, *Thoughts, Letters, and Minor Works*, ed. Charles W. Eliot, trans. W. F. Trotter, M. L. Booth, and O. W. Wight (New York: P. F. Collier & Son, 1910), 52.

But seeking out more silence is not just about avoiding damage, it's good for the brain. Two minutes of silence are more relaxing than listening to relaxing music,[8] releasing tension in the brain and the body. Experiments on mice found that two hours of daily silence produced new brain cells in the hippocampus, the area of the brain associated with learning, memory, and emotion.[9] If it did that for mice, what could it do for you!

Breathe In, Breathe Out

For many of us, these digital speed bumps may be all that's required to introduce more relaxation into our minds and lives. But let me add a couple of additional daily bumps you may want to explore. When I become really stressed out, I sometimes practice relaxation techniques. You can easily find YouTube videos and website articles that give you the basics of learning how to consciously relax your body from the top of your head to the tips of your toes. When I first did this, I was amazed to discover how tense my body had been and—surprise, surprise—how exhausted that tension was making me. Imagine going around with a fully flexed bicep all day, then translate that into the impact of a constantly tensed whole body all day. No wonder we often feel sore all over and generally fatigued.

Also, without straying into Dan Harris territory, you can

8. L. Bernardi et al., "Cardiovascular, Cerebrovascular, and Respiratory Changes Induced by Different Types of Music in Musicians and Non-musicians: The Importance of Silence," *Heart* 92, no. 4 (April 2006): 445–52; published online at National Institutes of Health, September 30, 2015, http://www.ncbi.nlm.nih.gov/pmc/articles/PMC1860846/.

9. Imke Kirste et al., "Is Silence Golden? Effects of Auditory Stimuli and Their Absence on Adult Hippocampal Neurogenesis," *Research Gate*, December 1, 2013, https://www.researchgate.net/publication/259110014_Is_silence_golden_Effects_of_auditory_stimuli_and_their_absence_on_adult_hippocampal_neurogenesis.

find many helpful articles and websites about how to breathe properly. "Learn how to breathe?" I hear you protest, "I'm alive, am I not?" Again, you'd be amazed at how poorly most of us are breathing, starving our bodies and brains of oxygen, leading to inevitable weakness of body and brain. Just taking one long deep breath from time to time lowers your stress, reduces your heart rate and blood pressure, and calms you down. Google "breathing exercises" and give it a try—just avoid the leg-crossing and the "umming."

Reading

The last daily bump I want to recommend is reading, which may sound strange given that we are trying to rest and relax the mind. There is something about reading, however, especially reading real paper books, that can be especially health giving. In "How Changing Your Reading Habits Can Transform Your Health," Michael Grothaus says, "Reading doesn't just improve your knowledge, it can help fight depression, make you more confident, empathetic, and a better decision maker."[10]

Grothaus's life was in a rut—until he read *War and Peace*. Its fifteen hundred pages took him two months to conquer, but it immediately became his favorite book because of how it changed him. "It's almost impossible to explain why," he says, "but after reading it I felt more confident in myself, less uncertain about my future. . . . As weird as it sounds, reading *War and Peace* put me back in control of my life—and *that's* why it's my favorite book."[11]

---

10. Michael Grothaus, "How Changing Your Reading Habits Can Transform Your Health," *Fastcompany*, July 27, 2015, http://www.fastcompany.com/3048913/how-to-be-a-success-at-everything/how-changing-your-reading-habits-can-transform-your-health.
11. Ibid.

But Grothaus's further research revealed that such a transformation through reading wasn't weird, but was "the norm for people who read a lot—and one of the main benefits of reading that most people don't know about."[12]

Grothaus's lessons have been confirmed by other studies. Researchers say:

- Reading for pleasure can help prevent conditions such as stress, depression, and dementia.
- People who read books regularly are on average more satisfied with life, happier, and more likely to feel that the things they do in life are worthwhile.
- In a survey of fifteen hundred adult readers, 76 percent said that reading improves their lives and helps to make them feel good.[13]

I try to set aside thirty minutes each evening for reading non-work-related books—usually biographies, works on history or fitness, *New York Times* nonfiction bestsellers, and so on. It's amazing how many fantastic books you can get through—maybe two or three a month—with just that short time every day. And for all my fellow type A's, remember that the point is not to chalk up "books read" or to use the time for sermon prep if you're a pastor, but to relax and enjoy.

Weekly Bump

Pastors used to be some of the happiest and healthiest people alive, with better life expectancy than the general population. But in "Taking a Break from the Lord's Work," journalist Paul

---

12. Ibid.
13. Alasdair Gleed, Booktrust Reading Habits Survey 2013, Booktrust, http://www.booktrust.org.uk/usr/library/documents/main/1576-booktrust-reading-habits-report-final.pdf.

Vitello reports: "Members of the clergy now suffer from obesity, hypertension, and depression at rates higher than most Americans. In the last decade, their use of antidepressants has risen, while their life expectancy has fallen. Many would change jobs if they could."[14] A 2005 survey of clergy by the Board of Pensions of the Presbyterian Church took special note of a quadrupling in the number of people leaving the profession during the first five years of ministry, compared with the 1970s.[15]

Vitello identified a number of possible causes for this change, including the added dimensions of stress caused by cell phones and social media, a reduction in the availability of volunteers in the era of two-income households, and the misperceptions that taking care of themselves is selfish and that serving God means never saying no. Most of the research, however, showed that the biggest reason is simply that pastors are not taking one day off a week.

Vitello's report confirms what I've seen, both in the United Kingdom and the United States. Pastors seem to think that "Six days you shall labor and do all your work, but the seventh day is the Sabbath of the LORD your God. In it you shall do no work" (Ex. 20:9–10) has an asterisk (*unless you're a pastor, in which case you must work seven days a week). No, this is a divine command for all, not an optional suggestion for some. God designed this pattern of six days of work and one day of rest for perfect people in a perfect world. How much more do we need it now in such fallen bodies in such a fallen world? This is a divine gift

---

14. Paul Vitello, "Taking a Break from the Lord's Work," *The New York Times*, August 1, 2010, http://www.nytimes.com/2010/08/02/nyregion/02burnout.html.

15. Cited in Ibid.

for our good, as Jesus said: "The Sabbath was made for man" (Mark 2:27). It's needed more now than ever before, considering that in the last twenty years working hours in the United States have increased 15 percent and leisure has decreased 30 percent.[16]

I confess that I have not found this easy. I enjoy my work so much that taking a day off every week sometimes involves considerable self-denial and discipline. I also see so much spiritual need all around that taking a day off sometimes makes me feel guilty. But I must obey God's Word, trust in the sovereignty of God, and reject my indispensability. I also heed Pastor J. R. Briggs, who says, "I have yet to meet a burned-out pastor who practiced Sabbath religiously."[17] One man asked me to emphasize that a day off means ceasing from all labor. He wrote: "I really thought I was taking a day off every week but what I was really doing was ceasing from one kind of work to catch up on another. I would cram my 'day off' with so many projects around the house that it became more stressful than my job."

My wife has been a huge help here because early in our marriage, she insisted that I take one full day off every week. A couple of times I persuaded her that I really needed to work on my day off, but by the end of the week, I was so mentally tired that I ended up getting less done than usual. The long-term consequences can be even more serious, as Wayne Muller notes: "If we do not allow for a rhythm of rest in our overly busy lives, illness becomes our Sabbath—our pneumonia, our cancer, our heart attack, our accidents create Sabbath for

---

16. Matthew Sleeth, *24/6: A Prescription for a Healthier, Happier Life* (Carol Stream, IL: Tyndale House, 2012), Kindle edition, locs. 6–7.

17. J. R. Briggs, *Fail: Finding Hope and Grace in the Midst of Ministry Failure* (Downers Grove, IL: InterVarsity Press, 2014), Kindle edition, locs. 2177–2179.

us."[18] One pastor who learned this the hard way looked back with shame on his previous 24/7 "deathstyle" and said: "I now had *one* day off per week. What a novel idea! Here I was, a full-blooded Sabbatarian by the letter and trouncing upon its spirit all along. I could now tell myself that the Lord's Day was actually a day of work for me, and so I was completely justified in taking Mondays off." As someone said, "It's not 'Rest when you have nothing to do,' but, 'Rest because we will never be done.'"

We need to see Sabbath not as something we *have* to do, but something we *get* to do. Peter Scazzero says that we should view it as God giving his people a snow day once a week.[19] It's a gift, not a threat. It's a time for healing the body and the mind.

Quarterly Bump

If you stretch an elastic band between two points for an extended time, it starts to fray until eventually the rubber disintegrates so much that it snaps. A life lived without relaxation is like that poor elastic band that is never released from its tension until it breaks.

One way to ease the tension that slowly builds and stretches our bodies, nerves, minds, and souls is to schedule "alone time" every three months or so, maybe a full-day or a half-day retreat. In a survey of solitude studies, Leon Neyfakh of the *The Boston Globe* explained that although many of us don't feel happy when alone, solitude results in better

18. Wayne Muller, *Sabbath: Finding Rest, Renewal, and Delight in Our Busy Lives* (New York: Bantam, 1999), 20.

19. Peter Scazzero, *Emotionally Healthy Spirituality* (Nashville: Thomas Nelson, 2011), 171.

thinking, stronger memories, happier moods, boosted creativity, more balanced personalities, and improved friendships.[20]

A retreat day should be free of all distractions, such as phones and computers. It should be focused on prayer, reading Scripture, and meditation, with the aim of renewing the soul and reconnecting with God. If Jesus needed this (Luke 5:16), how much more do we!

Annual Bump

Most of the men I've counseled through the reset process have neglected taking annual vacations, or they have fallen into the habit of mixing work with their vacations. We're not really relaxing if we're still emailing every day, calling the office, or preaching on the weekend.

A while after I persuaded one depressed pastor that what he desperately needed was a lengthy vacation, he wrote to me:

> I remember once reading Dr. Lloyd-Jones saying that every minister should have four weeks of vacation every year. I had guffawed. No way was I going to do that! I respected the good doctor; but deep down, I must have thought he was just a pansy. What hubris! Here I was now, drinking in every last drop of that four weeks of calm and renewal. I read a book just for the sake of enjoyment. The dissertation could wait. I enjoyed nature and just unwinding with the family.

Vacations produce a better perspective on our life and work, refresh our thought patterns, and renew our relationships with our wives and children. But above all, they allow

---

20. Leon Neyfakh, "The Power of Lonely," *The Boston Globe*, March 6, 2011, http://www.boston.com/bostonglobe/ideas/articles/2011/03/06/the_power_of_lonely/.

us to do nothing. In "The 'Busy' Trap," Tim Kreider says, "Idleness is not just a vacation, an indulgence, or a vice; it is as indispensable to the brain as vitamin D is to the body, and deprived of it we suffer a mental affliction as disfiguring as rickets."[21] "To do great work a man must be very idle as well as very industrious,"[22] observed Samuel Butler. As many have discovered, if we don't take time off, we will be forced to do so through ill health and lose more time than we ever imagined.

Seasonal Bump

In addition to these daily, weekly, quarterly, and annual rhythms, we should also recognize longer seasons of life that call us to adjust our pace. As Solomon said, "To everything there is a season, a time for every purpose under heaven" (Eccl. 3:1). He identified twenty-eight seasons (vv. 2–8)! Most of us will have fewer, but identifying our current season of life—getting married, having children, aging, bereavement, loss, relocation, and so on—and adjusting accordingly helps us to move wisely and confidently through each season at a grace-paced speed, with a calm and peaceful mindset.

We've just built a rather bumpy road, haven't we? But unlike most bumpy roads, this one will increase our comfort as we enjoy the benefits of quieter inner and outer lives, and build God-given rhythms of grace into our lives. The bumps slow us down, but they also build us up. They give us time to pause, to calm down, and to think about who we are and why we are here—questions that will be answered in the next two repair bays.

---

21. Tim Kreider, "The 'Busy' Trap," *The New York Times*, June 30, 2012, http://opinionator.blogs.nytimes.com/2012/06/30/the-busy-trap/.

22. Samuel Butler, *Further Extracts from the Notebooks of Samuel Butler*, ed. A. T. Bartholomew (London: Jonathan Cape, 1950), 262.

Rethink

↻

LifeLock, Identity Guard, ProtectMyID, ID Watchdog, Trust ID—all names we've become painfully familiar with through endless commercials on radio and television. Their ads follow us around the Internet, popping up here and flashing there, constantly reminding us that we are at terrible risk of identity theft, of someone stealing enough personal information about us to damage our finances and ruin our reputations.

The truth is that it's even worse than the identity theft protection industry portrays. Russian phishers, imposters posing as rich Nigerian widows, and Chinese hackers are the least of our problems. I'm talking about far more dangerous identity thieves that are far more difficult to detect. Pride, commercials, Hollywood, social media, parental pressure, success, disappointment, failure, the Devil, aging, bereavement, the church, and so on have been far more successful at stealing our identities than any online thieves.

But why are these identity thieves so dangerous? Because

they are stealing the answer to the second most important question in the world.

The Second Most Important Question in the World

If the most important question in the world is "Who is God?" the second most important is "Who am I?" Our answer to that question about our basic identities, the way we think about ourselves, impacts everything in our lives: our self-image, our health, our spirituality, our ethics, our roles and relationships, our careers, and our view of the past, the present, and the future. Answer it right, and we flourish. Answer it wrong, and we wither.

So why not get out your pen and paper and answer, "Who am I?" It's not as difficult as you think, because we're actually answering it constantly. Every day, each of us is designing and building an identity—a way we intentionally or accidentally think about ourselves (and how we want others to think about us too). To begin with, let's keep it simple: write down just one sentence or phrase that defines you. Let me help by giving you some examples of people I've come across over the years whose stolen identities affected their whole lives.

Andrew the Adulterer

After many years of faithful marriage, Andrew committed adultery while attending a conference away from home. Now, several years later, his constant magnifying of his guilt and his minimizing of grace mean that the first thought that pops into his mind when he thinks about himself is "I am an adulterer." That's his most dominant self-image, affecting his relationship with God and with his wife, and draining him of motivation and energy for taking on even the most basic service opportunities in his local church.

Fred the Failure

Fred spent five stressful years trying to plant a church in a large city. He followed all the strategies that the successful church planters have used. He bought all the books and went to all the conferences, but all he had to show for it were an ulcer, thirty to forty regular attenders, and a part-time job at Walmart to support his family—not exactly The Village Church or Redeemer NYC. Finally, he accepted a call to a medium-sized rural church that practically no one had ever heard of. He's appreciated there, he's well supported, his family life has stabilized, and he's seen a few people come to faith. However, as all he can think about is "I am a failed church-planter," he has withdrawn from his previous network, he avoids pastors' conferences, and he cannot rejoice in God's work in his new church. Another pastor with a similar story said to me: "When I resigned from the ministry I didn't want to be around other pastors (or anyone for that matter). I didn't know what to say to them. It was like my whole identity had been wiped out. I felt naked."

Simon the Strong

Simon's dad was a driven and successful man with high standards for his children. Illness was for weak people. Even when Simon was sick as a child, his father discouraged medications and pushed him out the door to school. He had to "toughen up . . . suck it up . . . learn to be strong." Simon unconsciously, though understandably, adopted this macho identity—strong, a driver, a hard worker—and carried it with him into adult life. Now, however, in his mid-40s, he's struggling to maintain the same level of energy and productivity. His mind doesn't seem to be as sharp or efficient as it once was, and he gets palpitations and chest pains from time to time. But because he is "Simon the Strong," he keeps driving himself, resulting in constant fatigue and frustration at his limitations.

Peter the Perfectionist

For Peter, everything has to be just perfect. It was the same for his parents. If he got 95 percent on an exam, their first question would be, "What happened to the other 5 percent?" Now, thirty years later, his inherited perfectionism has turned him into a hypercritical husband and father. It has also paralyzed him at work, as he finds himself unable to submit a report, make a presentation, or give a speech if it isn't close to perfect. Even when his boss or colleagues praise him, he berates himself for one or two shortcomings that he can't stop thinking about. As one man mourned to me: "No matter how much I accomplished I couldn't seem to focus on anything but my deficiencies. I saw myself as a failure. Somehow I managed to turn this into a spiritual gift. I imagined God being more pleased with me because I agonized over my flaws. It was a sick kind of penance."

Seth the Sinner

Seth attends a church that focuses mainly on sin. Justification, adoption, forgiveness, and other important doctrines are rarely mentioned. If they are, they are only postscripts to lengthy tirades about what's wrong with people, the church, and the world. He has little or no sense of God's love or of being God's child. His only thought about himself is "I am a sinner." He feels pretty down about himself and the future. His children dread family devotions and secretly call them "family depressions."

Justin the Just a . . .

I've met many Justins in the church. They usually answer my question, "What do you do?" with, "I'm *just* a plumber," "I'm *just* a salesman," or "I'm *just* a teacher." At the root of such answers is an unbiblical view of vocation, the wrong idea that only ministry callings are divine callings, that only overtly Christian work is worthwhile work. Justin has never been taught that "the action of a shepherd in keeping sheep . . . is as good a work before God as is the action of a judge in giving sentence, or of a magistrate in ruling or a minister in preaching."[1] If he had been, he would be a much more productive and happy employee and boss.

Mirror Image?

These are just examples of people who have had their true identities stolen by various events, circumstances, reactions, and decisions in their lives. In their place, they have substituted identities that are imbalanced and incomplete. In some cases, the way they think about themselves is completely false. Maybe reading about them felt like looking in a mirror. If not, I do hope you've now read enough to begin to recognize and articulate your own identity. Maybe you're Harry Hollywood, modeling yourself after the latest Hollywood star. Perhaps

---

1. William Perkins, cited in Os Guinness, *The Call: Finding and Fulfilling the Central Purpose of Your Life* (Nashville: Word Publishing, 1998), 35.

you're Frank the Facebooker, equating your identity with the number of friends, followers, and "likes" you have on social media as you shape and mold your persona there. Or possibly you have multiple identities depending on where you are and whom you are with! Whatever, take some time to ask yourself "Who am I?" and note the first word or two that come into your mind.

As you can see from the examples, and from your own life too, if you get the wrong answer to that question, it will have deep, long, and wide-ranging consequences. That's why recovering our true identities, and thereby thinking about ourselves correctly, is one of the core components of resetting our lives, of getting back on track, and of living a grace-paced life. That begins with recognizing our false identities and then rebuilding our true identities.

Recovering Our True Identities

Thus far, we've taken a relatively basic approach to identity by thinking of only the first one or two words that come into our minds when we ask, "Who am I?" That's because I simply wanted us to recognize that we do have a sense of identity and that this view of ourselves is highly influential in how we think, speak, and act.

Now we have to dig a bit deeper because none of us can be defined by just one or two words; we're far more complex and multilayered than that. So why not write down *all* the words that come into your mind when you think of the answer to "Who am I?"

To get you started, here are the words that came into my mind when I answered that question. I've recorded them in the order that they occurred: *preacher*, *pastor*, *professor*, *sinner*, *productive, father, husband, son, brother, Christian, skinny, good soccer player, principled, impatient, Scottish, introvert, reliable, Reformed, ill, technophile, political junkie, caring, a worrier, tired, independent, family-centered, a failure.*

Spend some time on your list—the first ten words or so will come relatively quickly, while the rest will take longer. And once you have your list, stand beside me and learn as I recover and rebuild my true identity following these eight steps: re-order priorities, expand incompletes, fill in gaps, prosecute falsehoods, add balance, reframe failures, accept change, and anticipate the future. This process will train us to think about ourselves in a more accurate and beneficial way.

Reorder Priorities

The first problem I notice is the order of my answers. Like most men, I have the tendency to define myself by my work—my work roles and responsibilities came to mind first. That's a problem for a number of reasons, not least because God defines people first of all by their spiritual state followed by their spiritual character. "The worst thing that happened to me in ministry," said Scott, "was when I forgot *who* I was in Christ. The second worst thing was when I tried to make what I *did* as a pastor fill that void."

It's also a problem because what happens if I lose my job, if I retire, or if my job does not go well? I lose my identity. Thus, I need to relegate the work component of my identity to a lower place and promote the spiritual component to the top of the list so that the most important and most permanent part of my identity comes first. If we follow the biblical order, we should first think about our spiritual state (saved/unsaved?) followed by our spiritual character (what marks of grace are in my life?), our relationships, and then our work. Whatever else was true of the apostle Paul, he knew that, first and foremost, "by the grace of God I am what I am" (1 Cor. 15:10).

There's more reordering to be done within these categories (for example, being a husband should come before being a father), but I hope it's obvious how the priorities of our identity impact our thoughts, words, and actions (or lack of them).

Expand Incompletes

The second step is to identify where some of these descriptions are incomplete and fill them out so that they are more influential in our lives. For example, I identify as "a *Christian*," but there's much more that can and should be said about that. Following the example of the apostle Paul, who found so many different ways to describe the Christian's identity in Christ in the opening verses of Ephesians 1, I can expand "I am a *Christian*" to "I am blessed in Christ, I am chosen in Christ, I am holy in Christ, I am adopted in Christ, I am accepted in Christ, I am redeemed in Christ, I am an heir of God in Christ, I am sealed in Christ" (Eph. 1:1–14). Do you see what a difference these additional truths can make to our self-image? The more words we use to describe our salvation by God's grace, the more influential this gracious salvation is for our sense of identity, and the more grace-paced our lives will be. A Christian friend whose functional identity had too often become "I am a sinner" and "I am a failure" found great help each morning by thanking the Lord using words he adapted from Richard Lovelace's *Renewal as a Way of Life*[2]:

---

2. Richard Lovelace, *Renewal as a Way of Life* (Eugene, OR: Wipf & Stock, 2002), 137.

I am accepted, because the guilt of my sin is covered by
the righteousness of Christ.

I am free from bondage to sin through the power of
Jesus in my life.

I am not alone, but accompanied by the Counselor, the
Spirit of the Messiah.

I am in command through Christ, with the freedom and
authority to resist the powers of darkness.

He also recites the following creed from Bishop Handley
Moule:

I believe in the name of the Son of God.

Therefore, I am in him, having redemption through his
blood and life by his Spirit,

And he is in me, and all fullness is in him.

To him I belong, by purchase, conquest, and self-
surrender;

To me he belongs, for all my hourly need.

There is no cloud between my Lord and me.

There is no difficulty outward or inward that he is not
ready to meet in me today.

The Lord is my keeper. Amen![3]

Fill In Gaps

When I came back to writing this chapter after a break, I
realized that there were some significant gaps, parts of my
identity that I had not included on my list, perhaps because
I did not want to admit them, as they involve some of my
besetting sins. But for accuracy's sake, I have to include these

---

3. Handley C. G. Moule, *The Second Epistle to the Corinthians* (Eugene, OR: Wipf &
Stock, 2015), 93.

significant weaknesses. For example, I am often *pessimistic*, *negative*, and *overly critical* (probably something to do with my Scottish genes).

On the other hand, I also left out some of my strengths. That's because I was given a very traditional Scottish Highland upbringing—you simply never talked about yourself or your family, especially if it involved something praiseworthy. To this day, I still find a kilted haggis on my shoulder telling me to "zip it" when I am tempted to put something about myself or family on Facebook or on my blog. But while there is merit in not boasting before others, there's no merit in ignoring the truth before God. Even though the apostle Paul acknowledged grace as the source of all good in his life, he still insisted that he was the hardest worker of all the apostles (1 Cor. 15:10). If God has given us a strength or an ability, it is part of our God-given identity; we should recognize it and thank God for it—though probably not on Facebook.

Prosecute Falsehoods

Not surprisingly, there are falsehoods in my identity. They are not easy to spot, however, because they have been so much a part of my being for so long. I may need help from an objective outsider to help me identify these lies, prosecute them, find them guilty, sentence them to exile, and then, using reliable and persuasive evidence, replace them with truth.

I am skinny. This might seem extraordinarily silly, but this is a massive part of my identity. I was terribly thin as a teenager, a fact not helped when I sprouted to six foot three inches, stretching my already meager frame even thinner. Boys (and girls) at school used to call me "the Cambodian" (there was a famine going on in Cambodia at the time, and images of skeletal children were all over the TV). Despite being a top scorer, I was denied places on regional soccer teams because it was thought I was too lightweight and would be too easily pushed off the ball. I used to dread swimming class because of all the ribbing about my bony chest and my pea-sized biceps. My skinniness even stopped me asking girls out for dates (probably a good thing, looking back). Recently, when looking back at photos of our honeymoon, my kids laughed their heads off at how skinny I looked at the poolside and threatened to put the photos on Facebook. It brought back some painful memories, memories that still make me hesitate before wearing T-shirts and shorts to this day.

And yet, however true it once was, it is no longer true that I am skinny, at least not laughably so. I can prosecute this falsehood by noting that I am now of average weight for my height. Second, my wife tells me that I have bigger muscles than I've ever had (that wouldn't be difficult). Third, I can favorably compare my bench press with other fifty-year-olds (and even thirty-year-olds). And I can even go to the swimming pool without hearing gales of laughter.

I am ill. A few years ago, I had a horrendous run of serious illnesses that fundamentally changed the way I looked at myself: a slipped disc, four surgeries, a double hernia, deep vein thrombosis and pulmonary emboli (twice in three years), diverticulitis, a kidney stone, and arthritis that dislocated my toe and irreversibly fractured my fourth metatarsal in numerous places. It is little wonder that I began to think and speak of myself as an old man. I was no longer young, vigorous, and healthy. I was falling apart, heading downhill fast, and probably needed to get my coffin prepared. As these self-perceptions filled my mind, I became more lethargic at home, stopped exercising, stopped playing with my kids, and just became rather morose and pessimistic.

Again, Shona has helped me get a better balance here. Without denying the reality of my medical record, she has helped me to see that I am actually quite healthy and still able to do far more than most fifty-year-olds. I'm on good medications for my blood-clotting problem, the arthritis is confined to one small area in my left foot, I go to the gym four to five times a week, and I'm stronger than I've been for probably twenty years. I may be a little ill, but I'm not entirely ill, and far more parts of my body are strong than weak. So "I am *ill*" should not be a definitive part of my identity.

Throughout 2 Corinthians, the apostle Paul prosecutes falsehood that had been spread about him. Clearly people were trying to pin a false and damaging identity upon him, and he is having none of it. He identifies the lies, proves their falsehood, and vigorously drives them out of the Corinthian church. This is what we must do in regard to our own identities.

Add Balance

I am a sinner. That's a truth, but it's not the whole truth. To be true to Scripture, I must also add the balancing statement "I am dead to sin" (see Rom. 6:11). Paul commanded me to think like this because the more I regard myself as dead to sin, the more dead to sin I will be. The next time I am tempted to sin, I won't simply cave because, after all, "I am a sinner." Instead, I will say: "No! I can't, because I'm dead to sin and alive to Christ!" Thus, I will die to sin and live to Christ.

A Christian man once confessed to me that he had been drinking so much that he had become an alcoholic and was attending an Alcoholics Anonymous group. He had a look of defeat all over him because he was constantly telling himself, "I'm an alcoholic." It is little wonder that, when faced with the temptation of alcohol, he usually succumbed. After all, he saw himself as an alcoholic. But however true that may have been, it was only half the truth. Imagine how much more resistant to alcohol's charms he would have been had he been telling himself: "No, I am dead to sin. I am dead to alcohol."

Reframe Failures

I am a failure. Yes, I just used the "F-word." Although over the last fifty years we've seen most previously taboo words "normalized," one horrific taboo remains in America: *failure.* There, I said it. And I've been it. You might have noticed that I put "*failure*" in my identikit. That's because I have experienced failure in business and in the ministry, and both failures have misshaped my sense of identity. I put it last on my list, however, because I've learned to view it through a different lens, as part of the "all things" that work together for my good (Rom. 8:28). I therefore no longer suffer from *kakorrhaphiophobia*—the abnormal fear of failure. I don't focus on failure and I don't deny it. But like many people who have experienced it, I do see it differently, and, like others, I have learned much from it.

For example, Apple founder Steve Jobs ascribed his success to reevaluating his life after three setbacks: dropping out of college, being fired from the company he founded, and being diagnosed with cancer. J. K. Rowling lost her marriage, parental approval, and most of her money. But then, with nothing left to lose, she turned to her first love—writing. "Failure stripped away everything inessential," she said. "It taught me things about myself I could have learned no other way."[4] As J. R. Briggs puts it, "Failure can be an enriching compost."[5] Indeed, "Ministry is fertile ground for failure, and failure is fertile ground for ministry."[6]

Learning to fail well is a vital part of the Christian life. A pastor said to me recently, "The first ten years of ministry is all about being broken and stripped!" I must have had a crash course, because it took me only five years to be broken, stripped, and branded a failure in the ministry! These were dark, dark days. Yet I know that my ten months in the school of ministry failure gave me my most valuable degree—a master's in how to fail well. As one man admitted to me: "I shudder to think where I would be today if God had not let me fail. My failures may have been painful, but unbroken success would have been deadly. Failure is one of God's greatest gifts to me."

If we have learned to fail well, we have realistic expectations of ourselves and our callings. We do not soar too high on success, and we do not sink too deeply upon setbacks. We take all our failures to our unfailing Lord for his full and free forgiveness, and we experience his unchanging and unconditional love. Then we reemerge—humbler and weaker, but wiser and happier too. And eventually we see how God can transform our ugly failures into things that are profitable and even beautiful. Breakdowns can become breakthroughs. When one pastor I know opened up to his congregation about his depression, he found the number of people coming to him for counseling greatly multiplied.

Here are some ways my failures have proved helpful to me:

---

4. Cited in Bruce Grierson, "Weathering the Storm," *Psychology Today,* May 1, 2009, https://www.psychologytoday.com/articles/200905/weathering-the-storm.

5. J. R. Briggs, *Fail: Finding Hope and Grace in the Midst of Ministry Failure* (Downers Grove, IL: InterVarsity Press, 2014), Kindle edition, locs. 76–77.

6. Ibid., 230–31.

My failures have drained my sinful self-confidence and filled me with sympathy for others. If I'd never failed in my parenting, preaching, teaching, financial decisions, and so on, I would have no patience, compassion, or help for others who have. As one pastor friend put it:

> I have realized that I've absolutely got to fasten my identity, like Odysseus to the mast, to Christ. My value is not in numbers or in outward success. But my success is in him who died and rose again, conquering sin and death. If Jesus wants to bless one in one way and me in another, who am I to talk back? "What is that to you? You follow me." And are there not so many other encouragements that God gives me? True, some have bigger churches—and bigger headaches. I have a small, but very devoted flock. Some have wayward children. While mine aren't out of the house, I have hopeful signs that God is at work. And probably, indeed quite likely, God is keeping me humble. If I saw tons of success, it would probably go straight to a self-righteous, bloated head.

My failures have helped to redirect my life. I've realized that I'm just not gifted for certain things I would love to do, and I should focus on the areas God has equipped me for. Though painful at the time, I can look back with gratitude for failures that changed my course.

My failures have given me time to think. The busyness of success is one of the greatest threats to peace and calm of soul, but failure stops us and forces us to reevaluate.

My failures have brought more glory to God. When things go well, I now recognize that it was God alone who enabled, helped, and blessed.

Above all, my failures have made me worship the Lord Jesus Christ more. When I consider how many minifailures I have in a week and how many major failures in a decade, I'm awestruck to think that he spent thirty-three years on earth and never failed once! He succeeded where I failed and imputed his success to me, so that I no longer see my whole identity through the lens of my failures. I've failed, but failure doesn't define me. I still fail, but he still loves me and accepts me.

Accept Change

We can cause ourselves huge problems if we do not accept changes in our age, abilities, capacities, status, and relationships. For example, in my teens and early twenties, I would have put "soccer player" at number one in my long answer, as my ambition was to play professional soccer. If I listed that as a primary part of my identity today, I'd be either lying or dying. Some men struggle to accept changes in their identities when they age, change jobs, experience ill health, or retire. Perhaps they try to work the same number of hours with the same capacity and intensity when they are fifty as when they were twenty-five; if so, they usually end up crashing and burning. But when God gives us grace to accept and adapt to changes in our lives, that is reflected in our sense of personal identity. We can then stop looking back with regret, stop envying others, and stop trying to live as if nothing has changed.

Anticipate the Future

It's sad to watch celebrities (and not-so-celebrities) vainly trying to hold on to their former looks and lives. They see that their best days are behind them, so they desperately try to recover and recapture those days. Models, singers, and athletes perceive that they are slowly losing their identities, what defined them, and will do almost anything to get them back. For Christians, however, our best days are ahead of us. No matter how well we manage to recover and rebuild our identities in this world, there is a better identity awaiting us in the world to come.

Consider the apostle John's words: "Behold what manner of love the Father has bestowed on us, that we should be called children of God!" (1 John 3:1). There's our glorious present identity: "Beloved, now we are children of God" (v. 2a). But however great that is, there's something even better ahead: "It has not yet been revealed what we shall be, but we know that when He is revealed, we shall be like Him, for we shall see Him as He is" (v. 2b). Imagine that! Our ultimate identity is not just to be *in* Christ, but to be *like* Christ! There is no greater identity in all the world.

So, yes, let's try to recover our stolen identity by rebuilding it on scriptural foundations: reordering priorities, expanding incompletes, filling in gaps, prosecuting falsehoods, adding balance, reframing failure, and accepting change. By doing so, we change not just our thoughts for the better, but our feelings, our words, and our actions too. But let's also anticipate the indescribable prospect of being like Jesus. If we add to our identity, "I'm going to be like Jesus!" it will have a tremendous present impact upon us because "everyone who has this hope in Him purifies himself, just as He is pure" (v. 3).

One of the great benefits of a clear sense of identity is that we can then more easily identify and clarify our life purposes and make plans to accomplish them, the exercise that awaits us at the next repair bay.

Reduce

C

I'd never felt so jealous—and I was looking at my two-year-old son. He was playing in the family room, jumping from sofa to sofa, climbing on the table, laughing and giggling with his brothers and sisters, and I so much wanted what he had—or, rather, what he didn't have. He didn't have a care in the world. He had no commitments, no deadlines, no worries, and no stress. I wanted that so badly again.

Life creeps up on us, doesn't it? At school, we just have school to think about. Sure, there are a few girlfriend and exam stresses here and there, but that's nothing compared to what's ahead. Fast forward twenty years and what do you have? You have college debt, a wife, teenage kids, teenage kids' friends, school sports, in-laws, two cars, a mortgage, insurance premiums, home repairs, car repairs, aging parents, nieces and nephews, a few friends, many enemies, a boss (or five), work colleagues, work conflicts, work meetings, work deadlines, work disappointments, church conflicts, church meetings, church deadlines, church disappointments, church services, money worries, and on and on it goes. The weight is piling on and your health issues are increasing. You're no longer making decisions that affect only you, but potentially hundreds of people. Now we're talking stress!

All that didn't happen the day after graduation. It accumulated imperceptibly, multiplying a little every year until life slowly yet inexorably smothered us. We took on a new commitment here, a new committee there; a new promotion track here, a new education opportunity there; a new counseling need here, a new service opportunity there. Now our minds are frazzled, our hearts are pounding, our bodies are breaking down, our relationships are straining, our sleep is declining, our quality of work is suffering, and our happiness is a distant memory. What happened to that two-year-old? Is there any way of getting back to that stress-free life (minus the diapers)?

Here in Repair Bay 7, I want to begin answering these questions by looking at two very different ways to live. This will give us a base to clarify our purpose in life, plan our days, and prune nonessentials, and so reduce some of the life-creep that has overtaken us.

Two Ways to Live

According to *New York Times* columnist David Brooks, there are two ways of thinking about life: "the Well-Planned Life" and "the Summoned Life."[1] In a column about this, he turned to an essay derived from a commencement address by Harvard Business School Professor Clayton Christensen for a model of the Well-Planned Life (WPL). Brooks describes Christensen as "a serious Christian" who "combines a Christian spirit with

---

1. David Brooks, "The Summoned Self," *The New York Times*, August 2, 2010, http://www.nytimes.com/2010/08/03/opinion/03brooks.html.

business methodology." Christensen's most important advice
to the students was to invest a lot of time while they were
young in finding a clear purpose for their lives. Looking back
to his days as a young Rhodes scholar at Oxford University,
he recalled:

> I was in a very demanding academic program, trying
> to cram an extra year's worth of work into my time at
> Oxford. I decided to spend an hour every night reading,
> thinking, and praying about why God put me on this
> earth. That was a very challenging commitment to keep,
> because every hour I spent doing that, I wasn't studying
> applied econometrics. I was conflicted about whether I
> could really afford to take that time away from my stud-
> ies, but I stuck with it—and ultimately figured out the
> purpose of my life.

Having found that purpose, Christensen said, we are then
able to make the right decisions about time management and
talent multiplication.

Brooks then contrasts the WPL with the Summoned Life
(SL), which is lived from an entirely different perspective. Instead of plotting a course like a strategic planner, we wait for
the course to unfold and respond accordingly:

> The person leading the Summoned Life starts with a very
> concrete situation: I'm living in a specific year in a specific
> place facing specific problems and needs. At this moment
> in my life, I am confronted with specific job opportunities
> and specific options. The important questions are: What
> are these circumstances summoning me to do? What is
> needed in this place? What is the most useful social role
> before me? These are questions answered primarily by

sensitive observation and situational awareness, not calculation and long-range planning.

So, which is the better way to live?

Is it the Well-Planned Life, in which we take time to find a clear life purpose, then make appropriate decisions about how to spend our time and use our talents? Or the Summoned Life, in which we reject the possibility of long-term life planning, but as situations and circumstances arise, we ask: "What are these circumstances summoning me to do? How should I react?"

As is his way, Brooks comes down firmly on the fence by concluding, "They are both probably useful for a person trying to live a well-considered life." He's right, but he doesn't offer any help about how to figure out when each applies or how much weight to give to each principle when making decisions about what to prioritize or what to prune. That's where I want to step in and take this helpful distinction to the next level.

Based on the truth that we are made in the image of God and therefore are called to reflect, to some degree, his purposeful sovereignty, I believe that every Christian should build on the firm base of a Well-Planned Life.

No Christian should be just a victim of events, a helpless cork tossed to and fro on the ever-changing ocean of circumstances and other people's expectations. God put each of us here for a specific reason, and we shouldn't just drift from day to day, from week to week, and from year to year, frittering away our lives without any sense of direction or jumping every time someone holds a hoop in front of us. We must take our time and talents to God, and ask him, "What will you have me do?" That simple prayer would have saved many of us from many years of pointless ping-ponging around from job to job, from passion to passion, from person to person, from church to church, from ministry to ministry, and from place to place. It will save us from spending our future days just responding to the never-ending summons of events, phone calls, emails, and others' agendas and problems, which creates huge stress and frustration for us as we relegate and neglect our primary callings and duties.

There are dangers, however. If we are living the WPL, we can become insensitive to circumstances, events, and people around us: "I don't care if my neighbor is sick, I have a plan and I'm sticking to it." We can become frustrated with anyone and anything that interrupts our plan or renders our day "inefficient." We can become deaf to God's voice speaking to us through his Word and providence as our lives unfold. Everybody must allow an element of SL in his or her life. As a pastor friend put it, "When my wife sees me frustrated at numerous interruptions, she reminds me that I have to adjust my agenda to God's agenda."

Consider Christ's life. He did not get up every day and wonder "What am I doing here?" or "Where am I going?" No, he had a very definite life plan (or, should we say, *death plan*), which he had received from his Father. He also had the right balance, however, between the WPL and the SL. While there were times when he would not be deflected by people's demands and the pressure of unpredicted events, there were other times when he did stop to respond to pressing needs and urgent circumstances.

But that was perfect, balanced, wise, and sinless Jesus. What about faulty, extremist, foolish, and sinful me? How do I balance the Well-Planned Life with the Summoned Life?

I have three words that, taken together, can help us work this out going forward: *Purpose, Plan,* and *Prune.*

Purpose

When we are growing up, life just happens. Food, school, sports, vacations—all seem to occur automatically. But as we mature and gain more independence, we have to start taking responsibility for these things and become intentional about them, or they just won't happen. We need to be purposeful.

Some life coaches encourage their clients to move toward a WPL by creating one single "life purpose statement" that is permanent and all-encompassing. This is then used as a governing principle when making decisions, setting priorities, and so on. The basic idea is a good one. The problem is that such a purpose statement usually is too generic and vague because it is intended to cover every area of life. Or, if it is made more specific, it ends up too long or fails to cover important areas of life. Also, it can be inflexible and unresponsive, incapable of taking account of changes that may occur in life. The frequent result is an irrelevant and forgotten life purpose.

That's why I suggest the development of four "life" purposes in the following areas: spiritual life, family life, vocational life, and Christian service. You may think of other areas, but you have to keep it manageable and doable. Also, I believe that these are the four most important areas to God and that this particular order reflects biblical priorities.

Spiritual Life

Who do you want to be? What do you want to be? What area of your personality or character do you want to develop? Or defeat? What do you want to stop being or doing? What grace do you want to cultivate? What sin do you want to conquer? These questions are focused on our spiritual development, our relationship with God, and our likeness to Christ.

Most of us, even most pastors, do not have specific aims or purposes for our spiritual growth. We just drift along, halfheartedly trying to try harder, vaguely hoping for some positive changes, but without any particular focus or plan. That means we rarely make much progress, and even if we do happen to advance in some areas, we don't notice it and take encouragement from it.

A sample spiritual life purpose statement might be something like this: "By God's grace, I will defeat anger and develop patience so that I might be more Christlike." Other examples might be: "By God's grace, I will defeat lust and cultivate purity," "By God's grace, I will learn how to pray better," and so on. A grace-paced life is a grace-producing life.

Why not ask others who know you well what they think your greatest spiritual need is? The point is to have a point, a clear spiritual purpose and aim.

Family Life

We can follow the same kind of process in devising a purpose statement for our family relationships—our marriages and our relationships with our children, our parents, our siblings, and so on. This might produce a statement like this: "By God's grace, I will lead my family to financial stability" or "By God's grace, I will increase the time I spend with my wife and children."

Vocational Life

For most of us men, the primary way in which we serve God outside the home is in our jobs. A purpose statement for our vocational life might be something along these lines: "By God's grace, I will learn how to manage and resolve conflict at work," "By God's grace, I will develop my leadership skills," "By God's grace, I will mentor new employees," and so on.

Christian Service

Remember, you are already serving God in your spiritual life, in your family life, and in your vocational life. That's a lot. If your season of life permits, however, you may also want to add a Christian service purpose statement something like this: "By God's grace, I will minister to the seniors in my church," "By God's grace, I will learn how to teach Sunday school," "By God's grace, I will evangelize one person a week," and so on.

Yes, we must be prepared to pause, edit, or even delete our life purpose statements and start over as "stuff happens" in our lives. But living our lives at the beck and call of everyone else is not living life in the image of God. One pastor who eventually resigned from the ministry for a time explained how he got into such a mess: "I felt like I was responsible to do whatever came along. I didn't plan. I reacted. I didn't know how to say no or what to say no to. My functional job description was 'Everything.'" If we have stated purposes though, we can use them to assess every opportunity and summons that comes our way.

Having goals saves us hundreds of later dilemmas and decisions about how to use our time, it prevents us spending most of our time fixing problems, and it helps those around us to flourish. In a survey of more than a thousand teams, Greg McKeown found that "when there is a serious lack of clarity about what the team stands for and what their goals and roles are, people experience confusion, stress, and frustration. When there is a high level of clarity, on the other hand, people thrive."[2] Working toward goals also energizes us by giving us a sense of progress and momentum. Above all, it helps us to die. According to hospice nurse Bronnie Ware, the most common regret of dying patients was "I wish I'd had the courage to live a life true to myself, not the life others expected of me."[3] I don't want to die like that.

Plan

It's not enough to have a purpose. We also need plans; we have to figure out the steps we need to take to get to our goals. If we want to strengthen our marriages, what steps will accomplish that? If we want to visit all the seniors in our congregations, how many a week will we visit, what time in the week will we do it, and where will we record progress? If we want to have more time with our teenage sons, where, when, and how will we do this? It's not going to happen without a plan. That's why I make sure that my calendar has time set aside each week for advancing my life purposes. If it's not on there, it's not going to happen. If it's not on there, I'm clearly not serious about accomplishing it.

Scheduling also helps us stop overpromising to ourselves or others. Overpromising is the fatal result of an overoptimistic

2. Greg McKeown, *Essentialism: The Disciplined Pursuit of Less* (New York: The Crown Publishing Group, 2014), Kindle edition, loc. 121.

3. Bronnie Ware, "Regrets of the Dying," *bronnieware.com*, November 19, 2009, http://bronnieware.com/regrets-of-the-dying/.

view of our abilities plus an unrealistic estimate of our available time plus a well-intentioned desire to please other people. The result is megastress in the one making the promises and usually huge disappointment in the ones receiving the promises.

Here are the stress-relieving steps I've taken to turn my purposes into plans.

Calendar

Shona and I spend some time each week coordinating our calendars, focusing mainly on the coming week, but also looking at that week in the context of what has gone before and what will come after. This prevents clashes, enables sharing of family responsibilities, and increases mutual accountability. We are especially careful to make sure that we are not out too many evenings in the week and that I am not accepting too many speaking invitations over weekends.

I never take on a task without estimating how much time it will take and entering that time on the calendar. For example, if I'm asked to write an article, I work out how long it will take me and then look for space for it on my calendar. If there's insufficient space, I have to say no. This works only if we consistently put everything that demands our time on our calendars—including family time, exercise, praying, and so on. Instead of saying yes to every request for our time, we get the calendar out and ask: "Where? When? Who? How?"

This might not be easy at first, but it's easier than the alternative, as illustrated by Bill, who explained his "conversion": "The concept of time management made me depressed. I thought it was a way that high-energy extroverts crammed more work into their lives. Now I realize it's a tool to help me focus on what I'm gifted at and enjoy. It protects me from myself and others who demand my time."

Routine

"Tell me your daily routine."

"Uh, I don't have one. Every day is different."

I can't tell you how many times I've had that conversation with burned-out pastors and depressed Christians. What came first—the depression or the chaos—is sometimes difficult to trace, but they seem to go together, each one feeding the other.

That's why one of the first things I do is to get them to draw up and commit to a basic routine of sleeping, worshiping, eating, working, studying, and so on. God is a God of order, not of confusion (1 Cor. 14:33), and as his created image-bearers, we glorify him—and feel much happier—when we live regular, orderly lives. He made our world and us in such a way that we flourish when our lives are characterized by a basic rhythm and regularity. That's why those who make the most progress toward their life goals are those who work on them at the same time each day or week. That's also why those who have the most routine in their lives are healthier and happier.

Professor Gail Kinman, an occupational health psychologist at the University of Bedfordshire, told *The Guardian* that, contrary to expectations, employees with the most flexible hours are also the most stressed, as their "always-on" culture makes it hard for them to switch off and keeps stress hormones persistently high.[4]

---

4. Juliette Jowit, "Work-Life Balance: Flexible Working Can Make You Ill, Experts Say," *The Guardian*, January 2, 2016, http://www.theguardian.com/money/2016/jan/02/work-life-balance-flexible-working-can-make-you-ill-experts-say.

Prioritize

"If you don't prioritize your life, someone else will."[5] If we want to do our own prioritizing, we begin by listing all our duties, activities, and aims. Then, using our life purposes, we put them in four categories:

1. *Definite do.* These are our most important God-given responsibilities and commitments.
2. *Desire to do.* These are activities we hope to do, and will do some of them after the "Definite-do's" are done.
3. *Delay do.* These are worthy activities that we would love to do someday, but which we have to postpone until we have space and time in our schedules.
4. *Don't do.* These are the things we either commit to stop doing or to say "no" to in the future.

Our life purposes and life priorities should then be reflected in our calendars, an exercise that usually reveals whether we are being realistic or idealistic. "Definite do" and "Desire to do" activities should occupy the most productive hours of each day. For me, that's seven thirty in the morning to one in the afternoon, and if I look at my calendar, I see, blocked out four days a week, "Writing" (that includes sermons, lectures, and books). Everything else connected with my work—administration, counseling, email, blogging, and other tasks—fits around that.

Using Steve McClatchy's helpful distinction in his book *Decide*,[6] I determined that writing is my primary "gain task," the one that produces lasting results, the one that will define

5. McKeown, *Essentialism*, 10.
6. Steve McClatchy, *Decide: Work Smarter, Reduce Your Stress, and Lead by Example* (Hoboken, NJ: Wiley, 2014).

my life, and the one that produces a sense of accomplishment and progress. In contrast, "prevent-pain tasks" are those that are not so enjoyable but which prevent pain occurring in my life (paying bills, handling email, going to meetings, etc.). We must prioritize gain tasks because they replenish us and because prevent-pain tasks just keep recurring. To summarize McClatchy, we need to overrule the brain's survival mode, which defaults us to prevent-pain tasks that deplete our energy, in favor of gain tasks, which energize us.

Audit

Every now and again, I write down each task that I do and record how long it takes me to complete. I'm almost always amazed at how long certain routine tasks, like making phone calls, writing emails, and such, take. Auditing helps me to schedule more realistic times for these actions in the future, thus relieving pressure.

Margin

If I think a task is going to take thirty minutes, I schedule forty-five; if I think it will take me three days, I schedule four; and so on. If it takes me less, I fill the time with something else that's useful—or I go fishing! If it takes the full time scheduled, I finish the job with less stress and I don't have to cancel or postpone anything else. It means operating at 80 percent capacity so that I can leave space for responding to unexpected people, problems, and opportunities. Another area in which to build margin is finances, and again, working toward living off 80 percent of net income is another huge stress reliever and health enhancer.

Review

I take ten to fifteen minutes at the end of each day to review what was planned and whether I accomplished it. I also take an hour or so at the end of each week to take a bigger-picture view and make any necessary adjustments. Initially, the comparison between the plan and the reality is a bit shocking, but slowly we align our expectations with reality, reducing frustration, disappointment, and stress.

Accountability

It is so good to have someone who speaks into our lives to say: "Why did you ever commit to that? How does that come close to aligning with your purposes?" Although I also bring speaking and preaching invitations to my elders, my wife is my primary accountability partner. She helps me to examine my motives for saying yes too often. I identify with this pastor, who learned this the hard way: "I had to come to terms with the painful reality that I couldn't say no, because I wanted to please people. I needed them to need me. I wanted to increase the number of people who admired me for being such a caring person. I was my worst enemy. I am thankful that God broke me so I could begin to break that habit."

Prune

A few life purposes not only help us to laser in on our priorities and make plans to accomplish them; they also help us to see that we must *remove* some things altogether in order to do the most important things well. Jim Collins found that "the undisciplined pursuit of more" was a key reason for most corporate failures.[7] In my experience, it's also behind many personal failures, especially ministry failures.

In our interconnected world, there are far more activities and opportunities than we have time and resources to invest in. Many of these are good, even very good, but few are vital. Instead of making a millimeter of progress in a million directions, by investing in fewer things, we can make significant progress in the most important things. That means taking the much-neglected knife of no to some branches of our lives. If you need that knife sharpened, perhaps you could make "I will learn how to say *no*!" your spiritual life purpose for the next year. It is a biblical word and often a biblical duty (Matt. 5:37; James 5:12).

Let's face it, how many times have we said yes to some request when every fiber in our being was screaming, "No, say *no*!" Yet, somehow, yes squeaked out. McKeown, who is a minimalism expert, insists: "The point is to say no to the nonessentials so we can say yes to the things that really matter. It is to say no—frequently and gracefully—to everything but what is truly vital."[8] Paradoxically, "an Essentialist produces more—brings forth more—by removing more instead of doing more."[9] Remember, it's rarely one extra big thing but the addition of lots of little things that tends to overwhelm us, because it is much more difficult to say no to the little things.

McKeown goes on to list a repertoire of ways we can say no, but they can be summed up this way: Ask for time and take your time. As he says, "We need to learn the slow 'yes'

7. Jim Collins, "How the Mighty Fall," *JimCollins.com*, March 2009, http://www.jim collins.com/books/how-the-mighty-fall.html.

8. McKeown, *Essentialism*, Kindle edition, loc. 1499.

9. Ibid., loc. 189.

and the quick 'no.'"[10] I do that by asking my assistant to send an initial holding response to most speaking, preaching, and writing requests. She lets people know that the requests will be reviewed by my elders, who meet once a month. This process not only gains time for prayerful consideration, it also helps the person or organization making a request understand that if no is the eventual answer, it's not just my personal decision.

Another area in which boundaries are required is in answering emails looking for counsel, guidance, book recommendations, and so on. Email has made us all so much more accessible, resulting in complete strangers beginning often time-consuming correspondence with us. Although I try to answer some of these, often sending inquirers to resource lists on my blog, most of the time I ask my assistant to send the standard reply, which goes something like this:

> Due to the volume of emails that Dr. Murray receives every week, many of them similar to your own, I've been hired to screen his email and answer on his behalf in order to free him to do the work he is called and employed to do at Puritan Reformed Theological Seminary and in the local church he pastors.
>
> Dr. Murray wishes it was possible for him to answer your question and give advice, but those who have a pastoral responsibility for him have decided that he cannot continue to answer all the email he receives and at the same time preserve good health and a good conscience.

It's not just single items we need to say no to. Sometimes we need to look at what has become regular and habitual in our lives and ask, "Should I keep doing this?" Some people

---

10. Ibid., loc. 1603.

find it helpful to have a "Stop-Doing List," often drawn up at the beginning of the year. We may have to prune relationships, expenditures, meetings, hobbies, or media. Less but better is the aim—the vital few rather than the trivial many. And the only way to achieve that is by learning how to say no. Richard Swenson lays down the challenge:

> Saying No is not just a good idea—it has now become a mathematical necessity. Without this two-letter word, I doubt that regaining margin is possible. If there are fifteen good things to do today and you can do only ten of them, you will need to say No five times. This is not rocket science but kindergarten logic.[11]

Just as we decide whom we will let into our houses, so we must decide what we will let into our working lives. Closing the door on some things is not selfish, but is a matter of self-care that ultimately helps us serve God and others better. As Peter Drucker said, "People are effective because they say 'no,' because they say, 'this isn't for me.'"[12] Less truly is more.

Magic Formula?

I said earlier that because we are all different and our circumstances are different, no magic formula fits all. What I can do is share with you the WPL/SL balance that has worked best for my character and my responsibilities, an equation that has helped me accomplish what I believe are God's plans for me while at the same time helping me remain open to interruptions and unexpected events:

---

11. Richard Swenson, *Margin: Restoring Emotional, Physical, Financial, and Time Reserves to Overloaded Lives* (Colorado Springs: NavPress, 2004), Kindle edition, loc. 122.
12. Cited in McKeown, *Essentialism*, Kindle edition, loc. 24.

70% WPL + 30% SL + 100% PL (Prayerful Life).

This doesn't make mathematical sense, but it does make spiritual sense!

We now have a renewed sense of purpose and a plan about how to get there, and we've eliminated some of the unnecessary baggage we were carrying. Let's now roll into the next repair bay and get refueled for the next stage of life's journey.

Refuel

C

I once asked a Christian psychologist how he treats people with depression or anxiety. "Oh, that's easy," he replied, "I give them three pills."

I inwardly groaned as multiple caricatures of pill-pushing doctors seemed to be sadly confirmed. After pausing for effect, however, he added, "Good exercise, good sleep, and good diet."

Our subsequent conversation made clear that he wasn't suggesting those three "pills" were the complete answer to every episode of depression or anxiety, but he was making the point that they are the fundamental building blocks of any long-term healing from mental and emotional ill health. As we've already covered two of these "pills," good sleep and good exercise, in previous repair bays, we're going to start this chapter by considering how the third one, good diet, helps to refuel run-down minds and moods. Then we're going to look at real pills, medications, and their potential role in refueling mental and emotional health. Last, we'll pour in some fuel supplements by identifying the activities that drain us and the ones that reenergize us.

Some guys might be tempted to skip this chapter because "diet is for women" ("I mean, I know how to eat") or because "meds are for wimps." Just as a Ferrari won't move without gas, however, and will be destroyed if we put diesel fuel in it, so we all need regular refueling with the right kind of gas if we are to run well. We've come a long way since entering the *Reset* garage and we've done a lot of repair work. But much of that will be in vain if we don't fill our tanks with premium gas. Our bodies and minds suffer from wear and tear, and they need to be reenergized so that they do not succumb to disintegration.

Food

I'm a theologian, not a dietician. That's why "The Murray Diet" begins with theology: "Therefore, whether you eat or drink, or whatever you do, do all to the glory of God" (1 Cor. 10:31). This profound Scripture verse tells us that there is a way to glorify God not just by what comes out of our mouths in praise and prayer, but by what goes into our mouths by eating and drinking. In other words, every choice we make about what to eat or drink either magnifies or minimizes God.

Our modern age has made this verse both easier and harder to obey. Easier, because we know so much more about the science of food and its impact on our bodies, minds, and moods. Harder, because there are so many more unhealthy foods and drinks to tempt us. That's why we begin implementing this verse by gathering scientific knowledge to educate our consciences and strengthen our wills. Consider the following food facts in relation to our minds and our moods.

Food and Mind

Research has conclusively demonstrated the impact of diet on our intellectual capacities and abilities. For example, did you know that the brain has more dietary requirements than any other organ in our bodies? It uses 20 percent of our oxygen, 20 percent of our carbs, and 50 percent of available glucose to do its job, much of which involves rebuilding, rewiring, and renewing. Here's a sampling of other recent findings to not only encourage further study of this huge subject but also to help us put better fuel in our tanks:[1]

- Skipping breakfast reduces cognitive performance because it deprives the brain of the nutrients, vitamins, and glucose that a normal breakfast supplies.
- Children who consumed lots of sugar and fizzy drinks in their breakfast diet performed at the same cognitive level as the average seventy-year-old in attention and memory tests. Toast, on the other hand, boosted kids' cognitive scores.
- Salads are packed full of antioxidants that eliminate damaging materials from the brain.
- Fish oil contains good fat that helps develop brains and wards off dementia by up to three to four years.
- Blueberries and strawberries boost short-term memory, focus, and coordination.

1. Most of the food statistics in this chapter are taken from Alan Logan, *The Brain Diet: The Connection between Nutrition, Mental Health, and Intelligence* (Nashville: Cumberland House, 2006). See also "Food and Mood," Mind.org, http://www.mind.org.uk/information-support/tips-for-everyday-living/food-and-mood/#.VvQQIZMrJTY; Sarah-Marie Hopf, "You Are What You Eat: How Food Affects Your Mood," *Dartmouth Undergraduate Journal of Science*, February 3, 2011, http://dujs.dartmouth.edu/2011/02/you-are-what-you-eat-how-food-affects-your-mood/#.VvQQ0JMrJTY; Joy Bauer, "Improve Your Mood with These Foods," *Today*, October 31, 2006, http://www.today.com/id/15490485/ns/today-today_health/t/improve-your-mood-these-foods/#.VvQPeJMrJTY.

- Avocados increase oxygen and blood supply to the brain (and lower blood pressure).
- Eggs are rich in choline, which produces memory-boosting brain chemicals.

When we pray "Give us this day our daily bread," God graciously answers not only by giving sufficient and suitable food for our physical *and* intellectual life, but also by calling us to take responsibility for the quantity and quality of food and drink we consume. We can't expect our minds to function well if we are stuffing our faces with junk. And remember, God works through our minds. He does us spiritual good by imparting truth through our brains. Thus, if we are not caring for our brains by giving them sufficient and suitable fuel, that will ultimately damage our spiritual lives as well.

Food and Mood

Not only are there many links between food and our *minds*, there are also multiple connections between food and our *moods*. What we eat affects how we feel. In a way, this should be obvious. If our food affects our thinking, it also affects our feeling, because what we think has a huge impact on what we feel. Food *indirectly* affects our moods through our thought processes.

But food also *directly* impacts our moods. For example, our bodies' blood-sugar levels have a big impact on our emotions. I see this visibly demonstrated every day in the life of my diabetic daughter. Although ordinary blood-sugar levels do not swing to such extreme highs and lows as they do for diabetics, we all get more cranky, fearful, and irritable when we go hungry for too long. Or, if we gorge ourselves on too much sugar, caffeine, or junk carbs, we are not going to be Mr. Happy (ask your wife).

But we don't need to rely on the evidence of our feelings or of anecdotes. Via PET scans, God is enabling researchers to actually watch the impact of certain foods on certain parts of our brains and the subsequent emotions that are generated. Some of the early findings are:

- Soluble-fiber foods, such as oatmeal, strawberries, and peas, slow the absorption of sugar into the blood, smoothing out mood swings.
- Foods such as walnuts, salmon, and vitamin D-rich foods increase the number and efficiency of neurotransmitters.
- Higher fish consumption, especially of tuna, has been linked to lower rates of depression and a stabilized mood (depression is virtually unknown among Eskimos!).
- Lentils and broccoli are excellent sources of folate, a B vitamin that appears to be essential for balanced moods and proper nerve function in the brain. A Harvard study showed that 38 percent of depressed women are deficient in folate.
- Junk food contains a type of fat that does not help mood but rather raises stress levels.

Now, of course, this science can be abused. Let's not start blaming all our bad moods on Dunkin' Donuts. Food is only one of many factors in our feelings. We cannot expect to have strong and stable emotional health, however, if we break basic nutritional rules that God has built into our world. So when we're down or anxious, let's open not only our Bibles but also our mouths. And when we do, let's turn to the salad bar rather than McDonald's, and reach for the orange juice rather than a Monster Energy drink.

Medications

Medications can sometimes help to replenish missing brain chemicals or stimulate the production of those chemicals and the connections we need for normal thinking or feeling. When I am counseling anyone with symptoms of depression or anxiety and the subject of medications comes up, I always make the following points:

Don't rush to it. Unless the situation is already desperately bad, usually medications shouldn't be the first option we consider. There are many other things we should do before resorting to meds (see previous repair bays).

Don't rule it out. Yes, we all would rather not be on any medication. And, yes, we should try other means first to aid healing and recovery. But meds should never be totally ruled out, especially when our reasons for ruling them out may be sinful pride, false presuppositions, or an unbiblical and over-simplistic anthropology. On that point, it's important to emphasize that a denial of the existence of mental disorders is essentially a denial of biblical anthropology in that it is a denial of the extensive, damaging effects of the fall upon our whole humanity. Our belief in such damage is rooted in Scripture and goes something like this:

Step 1: As a result of the fall, my body's physics, chemistry, and electricity are damaged.
Step 2: My brain uses physical structure, chemistry, and electricity to process my thoughts and emotions.

Step 3: My brain's ability to process my thoughts and emotions is damaged to the extent that my brain is affected by the fall.

Step 1 is a biblical fact. Step 2 is a scientific fact. Step 3 is the logical result of Steps 1 and 2. Other factors, such as childhood abuse, brain injury, aging, and sin, can increase the original inherited damage.

Don't wait too long. While rushing to meds is to be avoided, so is waiting too long. You may sink so low that it becomes much harder to emerge from the pit. The deeper you sink, the harder and longer the recovery.

Don't expect rapid results. Most antidepressants take ten to fourteen days to begin to make a noticeable difference and about a month before there's a significant improvement. There may be some trial and error involved as the doctor tries to get you the med that works best for you in the right dosage.

Don't rely on them alone. I've never seen anyone recover from any mental breakdown or emotional rundown on meds alone. But every person I know who has used medications as part of the kind of holistic package of care for the body, the mind, and the soul outlined in this book has recovered.

Don't dwell on side effects. Some people (a small minority) experience side effects from antidepressants. Side effects should definitely be weighed, but so should the side effects of doing nothing, especially the side effects on other people in your family. Sometimes taking meds can be an act of self-denial for the benefit of others around you. Take this brother's warning to heart:

In my circles there were plenty of horror stories about antidepressants. I heard the side effects were worse than the depression. I heard they didn't work or that they made the depression worse or that people became so dependent on them they could never get off. What I wasn't hearing (largely because I don't think those around me knew) was that there can be serious consequences for not treating some kinds of depression with medication. I damaged myself by going so long without getting medical help. That damage is still with me today.

Don't hold anything back. When you talk to your doctor, tell him or her everything. Let the doctor decide what information is relevant and what is not. Don't minimize or play down what you are experiencing; just tell exactly what's happening in your life and how you are feeling. You should also ask for a full physical examination, partly because living in crisis mode for too long can damage various parts of your body too.

Don't obsess about getting off meds. One of the most common questions I get from people starting antidepressants is "When can I stop them?" or "When can I get off them?" However, this angst about wanting to get off meds as soon as possible creates additional mental aggravation. My usual advice is: "Don't think about this question for at least six months. If things improve much quicker, then sure, we can talk about it, but for the moment, let's remove this unnecessary stress."

Don't come off them too rapidly. Although modern antidepressants are not addictive, it's not wise or beneficial to come off them suddenly or too quickly. Trust your doctor's wisdom and timetable as he guides you through a graduated reduction of medications over a period of time. If you get to a point where further reductions result in a recurrence of symptoms, however, you should return to the minimum dosage required to keep symptoms at bay. Some have become so run down and burned out that the natural production of vital brain chemicals will never return to full working order. (It's similar to running an old car on empty for too long—some of the sludge at the bottom of the tank gets into the engine, causing permanent damage.) In such cases, a small dosage of antidepressants may be necessary to top these chemicals up for the rest of life.

Don't be ashamed of meds. Just because some misuse and others overuse them doesn't mean you shouldn't use them at all. If medications are a good gift of God, we ought not to despise them. A grace-paced life doesn't reject any of God's graces if they are needed. One pastor confessed how he had been shamed out of taking antidepressants and then went on to shame others also:

> I was prescribed medication on two different occasions for depression but could never bring myself to take them. There was such a huge stigma in my mind about antidepressants. I had counseled people against them, even sending them books that argued against them. It took a great deal of suffering to make me open to them as a means God could use to help me. They didn't fix everything but they kept me from spiraling down while I worked on other pieces of the puzzle.

Try to view medications as a gift of God and ask for his blessing upon them. And pray for your doctor, that he or she would listen well to your story, diagnose you correctly and, if necessary, prescribe the right drug for you as part of a balanced package of spiritual, physical, mental, and social measures.

Don't tell everyone. With almost every other medication, you'd get lots of sympathy and prayer support. In the church, however, there's a lot of ignorance, prejudice, and misunderstanding around antidepressants, and you may not get much sympathy or prayer. You can probably tell which people will be sympathetic and supportive—usually people who have been through a lot in their lives—so you may want to carefully explore confiding in one or two of them. One man, who admitted that he had been simplistic and insensitive when it came to depression, learned about it the hard way: "I had no idea what depressed people were going through until I experienced it."

Don't believe the caricatures. Most depressed Christians I've counseled have not been losers or malingerers just looking for an excuse to opt out of life. Rather, they've been type-A hyperachievers who have burned out through overdoing it and are desperate to return to an active and useful life again.

Energizers

Good food refuels our bodies and minds. In serious situations, medications supply or stimulate additional brain fuel. Now let's identify which activities drain our energy and which refill our tanks.

When we were young, we felt as if we had unlimited energy; we just kept going and going, and nothing stopped us or slowed us down. But as we age, as the race lengthens, we begin to notice that our energy reserves are limited. There are times when we are flying; there are other times when we are flagging. Sometimes we feel we could run and run; other times we can't take another step. Often we just think: "That's weird! Yesterday I was cruising; today I'm crushed." But there's nothing weird or mysterious about it. Careful study of our lives reveals there is a cause behind every effect, a reason behind every reversal.

As I've grown older, it's become easier to make the connections, to link certain activities with feeling like a teenager again and other activities with feeling like I'm ninety. I've discovered that I start the day with a limited amount of energy and that everything I do either fills me or drains me; therefore, I have to maintain a balance between fillers and drainers if I am to run a grace-paced life. If I do only what drains me, I'll soon be running on empty and I'll putter out, often far from a gas station, needing a tow, and paying way too much for a refill. Through painful experience, I've learned that energy management is as important as time management, and therefore I must manage my fuel consumption much more efficiently than I did in my younger years. By learning what drains me faster and fills me quicker, I'm learning to plan ahead so that I can stop to refill my tank at the best times, places, and prices. Here's a sample of my own fillers and drainers to help you identify your own:

> **Fillers:** Bible reading and prayer; fishing; reading (mainly biographies and nonfiction from the bestseller lists); time with my wife and family; good food; writing; the gym; rivers, lakes, and oceans; preaching; political journalism; lectures that go well; close friends; seeing someone converted; growth in God's people; gratitude; laughter; etc.

> **Drainers:** meetings; pastoral visitation; conflict; criticism; fear/anxiety; counseling; busyness; overcommitment;

staying in hotels; conferences; socializing; late nights; talk radio; lectures that flop; email; dwelling on the failings of Christians; negativity; administration; etc.

Now let me give you a number of qualifications and explanations of these lists. First, unlike cars, no two of us are the same; what energizes me may not do the same for you, and vice versa. That's especially true when comparing introverts (me) with extroverts (my wife)—what fuels the one empties the other. Although the very sight of a piano puts me into "fight or flight mode" (due to two piano ~~torturers~~ teachers in my childhood), playing the piano puts one of my friends into mellow mode. He wrote:

> A good hobby is also important—something that replenishes you and that you do simply because you enjoy it. I took piano lessons from second grade through college and have always enjoyed playing the instrument. One result of my "reset" is that I have started taking piano lessons again from a piano professor at a local college—it has been invigorating and so relaxing for me!

This reminds us of the need to understand how we are wired and respond accordingly. One friend shared, "I am an extrovert who is energized by relationships and being with people," while another said: "I enjoy people but they drain my energy. For years I thought I needed to change myself into an extrovert. This was a disaster! I needed to learn to work with the way God designed me."

Second, I haven't included major life-event drainers, only the average daily-life drainers. For example, major life changes, such as bereavement, illness, marriage, divorce, job loss, work unhappiness, and others suck our fuel like a turbo-vacuum. Extraspecial care needs to be taken during such seasons, especially if lots of life events come one on top of the other.

Third, some activities could go in both lists! That's because even though some things fill us in one way, they may drain us in other ways. For example, although preaching replenishes me, it also depletes me. After spending a few days preparing sermons and preaching twice on Sunday, I'm mentally and emotionally good for nothing by Sunday night. So although I'm often energized by God's goodness to me in preparing and preaching sermons, and I'm often elated by encouraging interactions with people afterward, yet, on Monday, I have to take careful account of the previous days' rapid expenditure of gallons of fuel and compensate for it by doing things that refill me. If I don't, I'll spend the week just puttering along in mental weakness and emotional fragility.

Another example of this double listing is physical exercise—it obviously drains me at the time and for an hour or so afterward, but the net effect of it in my life is a huge boost of physical and mental well-being.

Fourth, although I've focused on the biggest daily drainers and fillers, I've come to realize that every activity, no matter how small or short, has some impact on me. As Brady Boyd warned:

> It's not big things but a thousand small things: This one little conversation, this one extra phone call, this one quick meeting, what can it cost? But it does cost, it drains yet another drop of our life. Then, at the end of days, weeks, months, years, we collapse, we burn out, and

cannot see where it happened. It happened in a thousand unconscious events, tasks, and responsibilities that seemed easy and harmless on the surface but that each, one after the other, used a small portion of our precious life.[2]

Our energy is finite. If we spend it on one thing, we cannot spend it on another. Replenishment must therefore be a daily activity, not something we do a couple of times a year on vacation and then try to live off for the rest of the year.

Fifth, if possible, I must fight to keep some drainers to a minimum. As one fellow adminaphobic told me: "Administration sucks the life out of me but I have to do it. It's simply unavoidable. But I also have a responsibility as a steward to beat it back as much as possible so I can do what God gifted me to do."

Sixth, although there are some things in my drainers list that I can work to avoid or minimize, there are others that I can't and don't want to avoid or minimize—they are important parts of my job and calling. I list them, not to say, "I wish I didn't have to do this," but to remind myself that I need to compensate for the drain.

Seventh, none of us should feel guilt for engaging in activities that fill up our tanks. If our tanks are empty, we are no use to anyone. We should be unashamed and unapologetic about doing what refills us. Leisure and spirituality scholar Paul Heintzman admits that "the word *leisure* almost never occurs in the English Bible. However, there are many scriptural themes that inform a Christian practice of leisure, including

---

2. Brady Boyd, *Addicted to Busy: Recovery for the Rushed Soul* (Colorado Springs: David C. Cook, 2014), Kindle edition, loc. 57.

Sabbath, rest, festivals, feasts, dance, hospitality, and friendship. These themes suggest that how we live our non-work time, the leisure activities we engage in, and a leisure attitude of receptivity, celebration, wonder, and awe are important to the flourishing of Christian life."[3] And who are good models for this component of the grace-paced life? None other than the allegedly killjoy Puritans. Heintzman explains: "The Puritans valued leisure for its own sake as well as for its usefulness for renewal; [they] thought critically about leisure as is evidenced by their opposition to blood sports, which were a form of cruelty to animals; advocated for designated days of recreation; and viewed life as a unified whole under God's sovereignty."[4]

Eighth, Richard Swenson warns about another three factors that prevent any gain: "Poor conditioning, sleep deprivation, and obesity constitute a physical energy desert where no margin can grow."[5]

Finally, unless you are happy at work, no amount of fillers will compensate for that drain. But the opposite is also true, as Steven Kramer discovered after reviewing anonymous diary entries from hundreds of people and covering thousands of workdays: "Of all the things that can boost emotions, motivation, and perceptions during a workday, the single most important is making progress in meaningful work."[6]

We now leave Repair Bay 8, having filled our tanks with good nutrition and energizing activities. We've plugged some

3. Cited in Tony Reinke, "Rethinking Our Relaxing," Desiring God, January 24, 2016, http://www.desiringgod.org/articles/rethinking-our-relaxing.

4. Ibid.

5. Richard Swenson, *Margin: Restoring Emotional, Physical, Financial, and Time Reserves to Overloaded Lives* (Colorado Springs: NavPress, 2004), Kindle edition, loc. 95.

6. Cited in Greg McKeown, *Essentialism: The Disciplined Pursuit of Less* (New York: The Crown Publishing Group, 2014), Kindle edition, locs. 196–97.

holes that were draining us and, if our breakdowns were serious enough, some of us have also taken on emergency supplies of medication. But since traveling is no fun on our own, let's roll into Repair Bay 9, open the doors, and take in some traveling companions.

Relate

C

My ministry has taken me to many places in the world, but no matter how exotic or beautiful the location, it always felt empty and hollow without my wife and children to enjoy it with me. In contrast, my family and I recently traveled to the United Kingdom to surprise my parents on their golden wedding anniversary. It was one of the most memorable trips of my life, not only for the joy we gave to my parents, but also for the joy of doing such a trip together, sharing in one another's lives. The joy of a journey depends so much on who's riding with us.

As God said, "It is not good that man should be alone" (Gen. 2:18). If a perfect man in a perfect world in a perfect relationship with God needed to hear that, how much more do sinful men in a sinful world in far-from-sinless relationships with God? It is not good for man to be alone. *Man.* That's me. That's you. Yet so many of us still try to live largely independent, solitary, disconnected, and self-sufficient lives. The result, as predicted, is "not good."

Central to God's answer to this "not goodness" was his provision of a wife to move the state of men from "not good" to "very good." But there are other key relationships in our lives we must consciously cultivate, especially in a fallen world, if we are to avoid "not good" and move toward "very good." Join me for some relational repair work in five vital areas: our relationships with God, with our wives, with our children, with our pastors/elders, and with our friends. Even if we just get that *order* of priorities right, it will make a massive difference.

Relationship with God

Like all healthy and satisfying relationships, our relationship with God needs time and energy. The good news is that if you have implemented the suggestions in this book up to this point, you have released time and raised your energy levels. But giving time and energy to our relationship with God actually increases free time and energy because it helps us get a better perspective on life and order our priorities better, it reduces the time we spend on image management, and it removes fear and anxiety.

Here are some things that have helped me to keep my personal relationship with God personal and avoid falling into the trap of relating to him only through my ministry to others:

Guarded time. I try to guard personal Bible reading and prayer time as jealously as I guard my own children. I keep my six twenty appointment with God each morning as zealously as if it were an appointment for kidney dialysis.

Undistracted mind. In a survey of eight thousand of its readers, desiringGod.org found that 54 percent checked their smartphones within minutes of waking up. More than 70 percent admitted that they checked email and social media before their spiritual disciplines.[1] I agree with Tony Reinke, who commented, "Whatever we focus our hearts on first in the morning will shape our entire day." So I have resolved not to check email, social media, or the news before my devotional time, as I want to bring a mind that is as clear and focused as possible to God's Word.

Vocal prayers. As I always pray better when I pray out loud, I like to find a place where I can do so without embarrassment. Hearing my own prayers helps me improve the clarity and intensity of my prayer. Also, I cannot cover up a wandering heart or mind so easily when I pray out loud.

Varied devotions. Sometimes I read a psalm, a chapter from the Old Testament, and a chapter from the New. Other times I read just one chapter or part of a chapter and spend longer meditating on it. Or I may read through a Bible book with a good commentary. Though the speed varies, I do try to make sure that I'm reading systematically through both testaments and not just jumping around here and there.

Good sleep. If I get a good seven to eight hours of sleep each night, I come to God's Word with more energy and concentration.

Christ-centered sermons. Using sites such as sermonaudio.com, I listen to many preachers outside my own tradition because I often find their approach to texts refreshing and stimulating.

Christ-centered books. Books that draw me into communion with Christ include John Owen's *The Glory of Christ*

1. Tony Reinke, "Six Wrong Reasons to Check Your Phone in the Morning: And a Better Way Forward," Desiring God, June 6, 2015, http://www.desiringgod.org/articles/six-wrong-reasons-to-check-your-phone-in-the-morning.

and *Spiritual Mindedness*; John Flavel's *Christ the Fountain of Life*; and, more recently, Mark Jones's *Knowing Christ*.

Selfish reading. Sometimes I read a book exclusively for my own soul. I resolve that I won't use it for any sermon, article, or lecture, and that I won't share any of it on social media. This makes a significant difference to the way I read and the profit I get from it.

Daily reminders. In order to maintain or recover communion with God through the day, I link regular daily habits with prayer or meditation. For example, I may use a coffee break to remind myself to pray, or I may use a time of standing in line to memorize a verse written on a card.

This personal relationship with God is so important because character is so important. Dave Kraft, author of *Leaders Who Last*, quotes statistics that show only 30 percent of leaders finish well, and in his experience, failures to do so usually happened because popularity and professionalism took the place of character in Christian leaders' lives. He writes that "in many quarters there seems to be a tendency to overlook a lack of character in one's personal and private life in exchange for a high degree of success in one's professional life. . . . Most leaders focus too much on competence and too little on character."[2] General Norman Schwarzkopf agrees: "Ninety-nine percent of leadership failures are failures of character."[3] Character is formed primarily in communion with God. We put this relationship first because it is the most influential in all other relationships, not least in our marriages.

---

2. Dave Kraft, *Leaders Who Last* (Wheaton: Crossway, 2010), 95–96.
3. Cited in James C. Hunter, *The World's Most Powerful Leadership Principle* (New York: Crown Business, 2004), 141.

Relationships with Our Wives

In the same month that Sandra Bullock won an Academy Award for best actress came the news that her then husband was a serial adulterer. Reflecting on this, *New York Times* columnist David Brooks asked: "Would you take that as a deal? Would you exchange a tremendous professional triumph for a severe personal blow?"[4] We don't like such questions because, although we would never verbalize a yes, our schedules and lifestyles sometimes say it for us. On the basis of extensive and rigorous research studies, Brooks argues:

> Marital happiness is far more important than anything else in determining personal well-being. If you have a successful marriage, it doesn't matter how many professional setbacks you endure, you will be reasonably happy. If you have an unsuccessful marriage, it doesn't matter how many career triumphs you record, you will remain significantly unfulfilled.[5]

Brooks also has a fascinating few paragraphs on the relationship between money and happiness. For example, did you know that "people aren't happiest during the years when they are winning the most promotions. Instead, people are happy in their 20's, dip in middle age, and then, on average, hit peak happiness just after retirement at age 65." But he returns to the connection between personal relationships and happiness, and concludes:

> If the relationship between money and well-being is complicated, the correspondence between personal

---

4. David Brooks, "The Sandra Bullock Trade," *The New York Times*, March 29, 2010, http://www.nytimes.com/2010/03/30/opinion/30brooks.html.

5. Ibid.

relationships and happiness is not. . . . According to one study, joining a group that meets even just once a month produces the same happiness gain as doubling your income. According to another, being married produces a psychic gain equivalent to more than $100,000 a year. The overall impression from this research is that economic and professional success exists on the surface of life, and that they emerge out of interpersonal relationships, which are much deeper and more important.[6]

Back to the deal: Would you accept a "successful" job (or ministry) at the cost of a happy marriage? If someone were to look at your calendar, would they know your answer to that question?

As there are many excellent Christian books on marriage available, and as the brevity of this book limits the space I can devote to this subject, instead of duplicating what you can read elsewhere, I want to simply share what has helped my marriage to Shona and hope that some of these thoughts may point you in the right direction:

Best friends. Given the choice of anyone to hang out with, I'd choose Shona. There's no one, male or female, who comes anywhere close to being a rival "best friend forever." We do date nights from time to time, but we're just as happy enjoying one another's company in the sitting room, in the yard, or in the car.

Spiritual fellowship. We're always talking about what God is doing in our lives and teaching us through his Word and works. That spiritual intimacy was the bedrock of our relationship at the beginning and has remained so.

---

6. Ibid.

Regular study. Although we've been married for more than twenty-five years, we still regularly read books about marriage. Sometimes we learn nothing new, but we always need to relearn old things.

Agreed roles. We follow the Bible's teaching on what kind of roles and responsibilities the husband and wife should have. However, as there can still be confusion or misunderstanding about what that means in everyday life, we regularly discuss who is responsible for what in order to avoid conflict or frustration down the road.

Quantity and quality time. I try to be home every evening for our family mealtime, at which all media and technology are banned. I try to be out no more than two or three evenings a week on church business. I take one full day off a week with Shona and our family (usually Saturday), and I limit my ministry travels to no more than six brief (two to three days maximum) trips a year. We take our full vacation time and make sure that arrangements are in place in the congregation for any emergencies so that I do not need to be contacted.

Frequent communication. Most evenings, we spend about an hour chatting about our day, our children, our challenges, our failures, and our successes.

Full accountability. We share our Internet browsing histories with one another using Covenant Eyes, and we share all passwords so that either of us can access any online accounts we have. We also check our bank accounts most days and make sure both of us are sticking to our budget. If I have a concern about Shona, I am not afraid to raise it with her, and she knows I want her to do the same with me. Nothing is off limits.

Same bedtime. We go to bed together at the same time, and the last thing we do every evening is pray together.

Lots of laughter. We try to make one another laugh, and if we've gone too long without a laugh, one of us will notice and say, "Hey, we need to lighten up a bit."

Vital vocabulary. The most important words in any marriage are: *please, thank you, I'm sorry, I forgive you,* and *I love you.* We try to say them as often as we can.

I remember an old pastor commenting that when a man tells him that he's struggling in his prayer life, the first question he asks is, "How's your marriage?" Almost always the man retorts, "What's that got to do with it?" The pastor then quotes 1 Peter 3:7, demonstrating the connection between a man's married life and his prayer life:

> Husbands, likewise, dwell with them with understanding, giving honor to the wife, as to the weaker vessel, and as being heirs together of the grace of life, *that your prayers may not be hindered.*

More often than not, the man then admits that things are not right with his wife.

We cannot expect to thrive or flourish if our marriages are withering. "The best decision I ever made was to pull back from ministry and reconnect with my family," said one pastor. "It may be one of the few things I have done for which I have no regrets."

Relationships with Our Children

I put this chapter on relationships toward the end of the book because until we put the previous steps into practice, we will not have the time, the energy, or the desire for the work that can transform our relationships from a burden to a blessing, from a source of guilt to a source of joy, from a drainer to a filler. That's especially true in our relationships with the children God has given us to father and pastor. If living too fast and too busily pushes our wives down our list of priorities, it usually drops our children off it altogether.

As with marriage, there are numerous excellent books on parenting in general, and fatherhood in particular, which I encourage you to read. (I try to read one book on parenting every year, even just to remind myself of what I have learned before.) Instead of simply duplicating what's available elsewhere, here's a quick list of the most joy-generating lessons I've learned (after much trial and error) in my relationships with my children:

God's fatherhood. I remind myself continually that I am called to represent God's fatherhood to my children, that I am the visible representation to them of God the Father.

Work-life balance. I'm increasingly conscious that my work-life balance is an example to them. If they see me living a grace-paced life in a burnout culture, there is far greater hope of them doing the same.

Gospel. I not only teach them the gospel and make sure they hear it each week in a faithful local church, but I also try to live it out by practicing grace in my relationships with them and by continually pointing them to Christ for forgiveness when they fail and to the Holy Spirit for strength when they are weak.

Humility. When I sin against them in my parenting, I ask them for forgiveness as soon as possible. I have never regretted saying "I'm sorry" to my children. And I've said it too many times to count.

Patience. If I've learned anything over twenty years of parenting five children, it is to be patient, to be long-suffering and slow to anger, to persevere through disappointments, and to wait in faith for lessons to be learned and for their lives to be changed.

Time. As with marriage, there is simply no substitute for time with our children. In addition to eating with them and leading family worship as many evenings a week as I can, I devote my days off to my wife and children. I very rarely go off and do something on my own or with friends. We put a lot of effort into taking vacations together. I bought a small boat so that we can fish and explore Michigan's lakes and rivers together. We ski and snowboard together each winter. We limit our teenagers to three nights out a week apart from Sunday, when they go to youth group.

Encouragement. I look for and take every opportunity to encourage them in their faith, in their schoolwork, in their sports, in their appearance, and in their friendships. I try to make sure that the encouragement-to-criticism ratio is something like 5:1.

Clarity. I've found that my children thrive when Shona and I lay down clear and consistent rules and boundaries for them. They may not like it at first, and it sometimes takes much faith to follow through, but it has always worked out for the best.

Worship. We prioritize family worship and are continually adjusting our evening schedule to make sure the maximum number of our children is present for it each day.

When we are stressed and tired, spending time and doing things with our children can feel like just one other to-do, another drainer. However, I've found that when I am rested and have margin in my life, the same activities that previously were drainers can become fillers and energizers.

Relationships with Our Pastors/Elders

We need official spiritual oversight in our lives. This is especially true for pastors, not only because they are special targets of the Evil One, but also because there is a tragic epidemic of leadership falls among Christian leaders. In every case that I know of—and there are more than I want to count—the common feature is a reluctance to be accountable, a pulling away from the oversight of other pastors and elders. As I write this, just in the past two days, I have heard of one young pastor/missionary, one middle-aged celebrity pastor, and one older pastor nearing the end of his ministry who have fallen into the sin of adultery. All had left institutions and denominations in the past two to three years to "do their own ministry," to operate more or less independently of any oversight or accountability. All ended up in illicit relationships with women, partly because they rejected a biblical relationship with the local church and became spiritual "Lone Rangers."

Although recent LifeWay research has debunked the myth of twelve hundred pastors leaving the ministry every month,[7] another one of its surveys found that due to the burden of ministry, many pastors do struggle with mental illness. Twenty-three percent say they've experienced some kind of mental illness, while 12 percent have received a diagnosis for a mental-health condition.[8] However, the study also found

---

7. Ed Stetzer, "Despite Wrong Doomsday Stats, Pastors Holding Up Just Fine," *Christianity Today*, November 6, 2015, http://www.christianitytoday.com/edstetzer/2015/november/despite-wrong-doomsday-stats-pastors-holding-up-just-fine.html.

8. Ibid., citing Bob Smietana, "Mental Illness Remains Taboo Topic for Many Pastors," LifeWay Research, September 22, 2014, http://lifewayresearch.com/2014/09/22/mental-illness-remains-taboo-topic-for-many-pastors/.

that they are often reluctant to share their struggles. Ed Stetzer says: "It's important for pastors to be able to be open with co-laborers about their struggles when possible and in appropriate ways. Without the permission or ability to be open about the struggles that come along with a life in ministry, pastors are going to be more prone to burnout or quitting altogether. The church must be understanding of this struggle and support their pastors as they are able."[9]

We all need men in our lives who deal lovingly and faithfully with us, who watch for our souls and speak into our lives when we need that. Although this requires us to make ourselves vulnerable, and that takes tremendous courage, doing so is a wise and safe act, especially as we mature or succeed and perhaps become more self-confident and self-sufficient.

Relationships with Our Friends

The last passengers we need for our journey are friends, a relationship in which few men excel. Why do we fail so badly here?

We're too busy. Deep friendships take time, lots of time doing nothing terribly productive, but just being together, talking, and listening. Who has time for that in today's busy world?

We're too selfish. Male friendships are too often based on what we can sell to someone or what we can get from someone. "What's in it for me?" is too often the primary or only criterion for whether we build a relationship with someone.

We're too functional. Male friendship usually grows out of organizations—work, sports, clubs, and so on. The problem

---

9. Ibid.

is that if our participation ends, so do our friendships. They are more functional than emotional. True friendship involves being around people just for their own sake.

We're too proud. "Friends are for wimps!" OK, we might not say it, but we often think it. "I'm strong, independent, self-sufficient. I can manage life on my own. I don't need friends."

We're too safe. We're not prepared to risk rejection. It seems better to stay in the safety zone of arms-length acquaintance than try to get closer and risk seeing someone back off or push off. That's why 90 percent of American men have never known a relationship in which they could be truly vulnerable and open.

We're too superficial. Friendships can thrive only where there is real authenticity, where both parties are prepared to let down their guard and show their real emotions and feelings. That requires going beyond the superficial self-images that we build up.

We're too brainwashed. Most of us have taken our view of masculinity from TV and Hollywood. Mark Greene wrote:

> A real man is strong and stoic. He doesn't show emotions other than anger and excitement. He is a breadwinner. He is heterosexual. He is able-bodied. He plays or watches sports. He is the dominant participant in every exchange. He is a firefighter, a lawyer, a CEO. He is a man's man. This "real man" . . . represents what is supposedly norma- tive and acceptable within the tightly controlled perfor- mance of American male masculinity.[10]

10. Mark Greene, "Why Men Have So Much Trouble Making Friends," *Salon*, April 12, 2014, http://www.salon.com/2014/04/12/why_do_mens_friendships_feel_so_hollow _partner/.

What, then, is the solution to this friendship failure? As usual, the solution begins with theology, especially the nature of God. God exists as a united community of three persons in intimate relationship, and he calls us to be his image-bearers in pursuing relationship and community with others. We can turn that biblical theology into practical theology by studying Jesus Christ, the friend of sinners in general, but also a man who built twelve strong male friendships in just a few short years, friendships that were motivated by a desire to do eternal and spiritual good for these varied and faulty men. He solved problems not by throwing money around or by setting up classes, but by loving people.

Making Biblical Friendships

Building on the work of Jonathan Holmes in *The Company We Keep: In Search of Biblical Friendship*,[11] here are some helps to cultivating biblical friendships:

Prioritize friendships. If we don't make healthy friendships a goal, they won't happen. Motivate yourself with the *advantages*, including less depression and better immune systems.[12] Alan McGinnis writes:

> In my work as a psychotherapist . . . , I have become more convinced than ever that a restoring and renewing power resides in friendship. If people availed themselves of the love available to them, many therapists like me could close up shop.[13]

---

11. Jonathan Holmes, *The Company We Keep: In Search of Biblical Friendship* (Minneapolis: Cruciform Press, 2014).
12. Matthew Edlund, *The Power of Rest: Why Sleep Alone Is Not Enough* (New York: HarperCollins, 2010), Kindle edition, loc. 2275.
13. Alan Loy McGinnis, *The Friendship Factor* (Minneapolis: Fortress Press, 2003), Kindle edition, loc. 95.

Motivate yourself also with the *disadvantages* of isolation. For example, lonely people live shorter lives and suffer more ill health.[14] Scientists from the University of North Carolina examined the relationship between friendship and health at different life stages and found that loneliness can "vastly elevate" a person's risk of heart disease, stroke, and cancer.[15] One long-term Harvard study of students who never achieved financial success or even reached middle management found that the common factor was that not one had achieved intimacy, as reflected by stable marriages and lasting friendships. In general, there was a direct correlation between the amount of love in their personal lives and the amount of success they had in the outside world.[16]

Cultivate the greatest friendship. Without an understanding of Christ's friendship with us, we will either never make friends, we will make them for all the wrong reasons, or we will end friendships quickly. His friendship with us, so patient, so full of grace, so full of forgiveness, must be the model for our friendships with others.

Build unselfish friendships. Make sure you have a friendship or two that does not help your career or build your network.

Beware of substitutes. Social media might begin a friendship, but rarely does it constitute a friendship. British Institute fellow Aric Sigman has found that "face-to-face communications involve very different brain circuitry than virtual ones."

---

14. Ibid., loc. 8–9.
15. Yang Claire Yang et al., "Social Relationships and Physiological Determinants of Longevity across the Human Life Span," *Proceedings of the National Academy of Sciences of the United States of America*, July 20, 2015, http://www.pnas.org/content /113/3/578.abstract.
16. McGinnis, *The Friendship Factor*, Kindle edition, loc. 18–19.

He quoted Duke University research from 2005 that found that in the previous twenty years, with the rise of virtual communications, the number of people who said they had no one with whom to discuss serious personal matters increased from 7 percent to 25 percent.[17]

Prepare for disappointments. If you pursue biblical friendships, you will get unbiblical rejections! You will get misunderstanding, rejection, and betrayal. But you will also get one or two really good friends who will be worth all the pain along the way. It's worth persevering.

Cultivate transparency. One of the best definitions of friendship I've heard is "to know and be known." Pretense, show, and every other mask is removed by both parties as they say to one another, "This is the real me." See the benefits of such openness in this testimony: "God has blessed me with some terrific friends. They have been key to my renewal of strength and joy over the last half year. I would really encourage any pastors who are struggling with depression to open up to some key friends as soon as possible." That means honesty about our struggles, as this friend's story illustrates: "I have been amazed at how many men will open up about struggles when they know it's safe. The way they know it's safe is when they hear me talk about my own struggles. So many of us are starving for transparency. We are tired of putting up the façade. It's not healthy."

Make spiritual growth central. Male friendship can involve sports, games, hobbies, helping one another with practical problems, laughing, storytelling, and many other beautiful gifts of God. But it must have at its core a desire to do spiritual

---

17. Cited in Edlund, *The Power of Rest*, Kindle edition, loc. 2305.

good to one another. Regularly ask one another questions like these: "How can I pray for you? Where are you struggling? Where have you experienced God's grace in your struggle? What is bringing joy to your heart? Where do you see me growing spiritually? How can I be a better friend to you?"[18]

Recognize your limitations. You can't be friends with everyone. Jesus had twelve friends, three special friends, and one unique friend. If we can achieve that, we're doing really well. At times, we need to prune friendships, and at other times, we need to establish clearer borders.

Revving Up and Raring to Go

We've done a ton of repair work. Our tank is full of gas and our vehicle is full of passengers. Our relationships with our passengers—God, our wives, our children, our pastors and elders, and our friends—are in much healthier shape. Now, let's roll on to the last repair bay to rev up our engines and get ready to reenter the race. This time, however, it will be grace-paced, not rocket-charged.

---

18. Holmes, *The Company We Keep*, Kindle edition, loc. 69.

Resurrection

↻

Every one of the men I've coached through *Reset* garage has left it deeply thankful to God for bringing them into it. No matter how reluctantly they entered it, they all thank God for the experience, not only for the various repairs, but also for the prospect of a new and better life than they were leading before. Some of them have compared it to a miniresurrection, a little taste or sample of what the ultimate resurrection will be like when we leave all things of death behind and experience all things new.

Yes, we have bad memories of the old ways that damaged us—the debilitating stress, unrealistic expectations, dark depression, crashed morals, and burned-out souls—all of which cause some hesitation and fear about returning to the race. But the abundance of newness and grace encourages us forward.

The new ways that have been built into your life in the *Reset* garage may include some or all of the following:

New Pace

The verse above the garage exit reads: "Do you not know that those who run in a race all run, but one receives the prize? Run in such a way that you may obtain it" (1 Cor. 9:24). When we read that verse before entering the garage, all we could think of was a hundred-meter sprint and running as fast as we could all the time. But we've learned that life is better viewed as a long-distance race, and that quite a different pace, as well as different skills and tactics, is required to run it, enjoy it, finish it, and win it.

Yes, there will be crisis times when we have to up our tempo and expend more energy, when we have to work longer and harder than our new normal, but that occasionally increased pace will no longer be our lifestyle. Also, such emergencies will not damage us as much as before because we've built margin into our lives for unexpected busyness, stress, and problems.

New Conscience

Initially, we can expect some difficulty as we slow our pace. It may be difficult for us because, in comparison with our pre-*Reset* lives, we may feel lazy to be running slower, or we may feel guilty about reducing other commitments and taking breaks to renew our energy. When such false guilt creeps up behind us, taps our shoulders, and whispers "Faster" in our ears, we must educate our consciences with the biblical knowledge and understanding gained in *Reset* garage. This process of reeducating the conscience was illustrated in Stephen's note to me:

> I came to the point where I realized I had to fight false guilt with true guilt. I wrongly felt guilty because I couldn't be everything to everyone all the time. Instead, I needed to

feel guilty for trying to be God. I needed to feel guilty for not submitting to the limits he placed me under. My problem was basically the same as someone living beyond their financial means. I was overspending. I had convinced myself God wanted me to. I made his yoke hard and his burden heavy.

New Honesty

Our new pace may be difficult for those around us, who are used to our previously faster pace and greater capacity. Honest conversations with our wives, our kids, our pastors, our elders, our colleagues, and others may be required to explain the adjustments we've had to make to our lives and work due to aging and other factors. We can't expect everyone to understand immediately and sympathize completely, but we must act in faith that this is the right thing to do for us and for them. Also, I've been surprised at how many men have seen my own admission of weakness and vulnerability, then have used that to give themselves permission to be weak and tired, and to make their own life-enhancing and ministry-extending adjustments.

New Contentment

In a blog post titled "A Marathon Mentality for Ministry," pastor Nick Batzig points to the apostle Paul languishing in a Roman prison, yet writing Philippians 4:11–13, and notes: "Contentment in ministry is a secret of endurance in ministry. Pastors must learn to be content with what hand God has dealt them."[1] Part of this contentment is derived from biblical

---

1. Nick Batzig, "A Marathon Mentality for Ministry," *Christward Collective*, March 17, 2016, http://www.alliancenet.org/christward/a-marathon-mentality-for-ministry#.VvAUn5MrJcA.

measures of faithfulness and fruitfulness rather than cultural standards. The same goes for nonministry callings too.

New Selectivity

We're not only running at a slower pace, we're also running in fewer but better races. We've surveyed our lives and decided which races God wants us to run, what life purposes he wants us to fulfill. Instead of being pushed and pulled in a hundred directions, running races that we've thoughtlessly drifted into, we have purposed, planned, and pruned, so that we say no to multiple other possible races—many of them good and noble, but not our races to run.

New Energy

Our slower pace uses less fuel, and better fuel, and also drains it more slowly. We're no longer swinging from hyperactive to hyperexhausted, and we're no longer trying to run on fumes plus willpower. We've learned what drains us and what refills us. We eat and drink better, and we know when to relax the pace, when to take a rest, and when to get help from other team members. All in all, we now run with more energy and pleasure on cleaner and healthier fuel.

New Joy

What excites me most about resetting men's lives is seeing the new joy with which they now run their races. When I first see them, they are depressed, discouraged, depleted, and often despairing. They are looking at the track ahead and saying, "I can't run another lap," or, in some cases, "I can't take another step." They have no hope of a better future and little expectation of beneficial change. Some want to end their races altogether; a few have even thought of ending their lives.

But as they move through the garage, I see flickers of hope, I hear laughter again, and I sense a new joy in their work and in their marriages. Eventually they look up and see good things ahead, and can even face the bad things with faith instead of fear. Their wills are strengthened so that duties they dreaded and avoided become doable. Their new eating and exercise habits are boosting their physical and emotional health. Free time, days off, and vacations no longer induce guilt, shame, and defensiveness, but are received as gifts of a gracious God, the new center of their new joy. They have a new intimacy with him, a new dependence on him, a new view of him, and a new enjoyment of him.

New Theology

So much of our drivenness stems from a false belief in a driven God, a view of God as a slaveholder, a harsh taskmaster who can never be satisfied by anything less than his people being in a perpetual state of miserable exhaustion. But now, with a focus on God as a loving heavenly Father, as a slave emancipator, as gracious, as delighting in his people, as the happy giver of all good gifts to his children, as the rester and refresher of his people, as the feeder and waterer of his sheep, not only does God look different, but the whole world does—including the person in the mirror. Yes, we still desire to serve God to the full, but there's much more resting in God and delighting in God. There's a deep embrace and enjoyment of the gospel of rest that is not only understood with our minds and spoken with our lips, but also demonstrated in peaceful, calm lives of total trust in the God of peace.

New Team

I've learned through painful experience that I must run as part of a team. I need others to run alongside me, to encourage me, to keep me accountable, to direct me, and, sometimes, to carry me.

Here again, it's been a joy to see the *Reset* process resurrect vital relationships in my life and in the lives of other men I've coached. Marriages have been revived, fathering has been rejuvenated, spiritual accountability to pastors and elders has been resuscitated, and deep male friendships have been initiated and revitalized as life was shared and lived in vibrant community, especially in the local church. Pastor Doug told me excitedly: "I've been working very hard at building up a cross-functional team in ministry here. I've been open about not being able to do everything—and I've found that by empowering other people, it increases their joy and enhances my own happiness and peace."

New Sensitivity

Reset garage produces a much better and humbler understanding of our humanity. We now keep our eyes on the dashboard and know which warning lights to look out for and what they mean—warning signs that we previously would have ignored, minimized, or resented. We're sensitive to physical, mental, emotional, spiritual, and relational changes, and collaborate more knowledgeably with the biological rhythms of our bodies. We sense the monthly mix, the weekly beat of six days of work and one day of rest, the daily cadence of work and sleep, the regular tempo of hunger and thirst, and even the pulses of dynamic energy that peak a few times a day, enabling us to find our flow state and do our best work. Going forward, we are much more attuned to this God-given rhythm, and, instead of fighting it, we have gotten with the groove and beat of God's order in our lives.

Our experiences have also given us a sensitivity to the danger that others are in, as evidenced by this appeal of one man who has been through *Reset* garage:

> I write this after close to two of the most unexpected years of my life. Much of these two years has been checkered, and some parts of it were a small taste of hell. But Christ has brought me through. I am still learning. And I am a very slow learner. But I am back in the race, slower, but more confident that I will eventually cross the finish line. I await the crown, earned not by me but by my blessed Savior. But I run with greater caution. And I hope my story serves as a wakeup call to other runners who may be outpacing me now, but are running on empty. Don't let me see you sprawled out on the sideline, with medics rushing to your side. Believe me, it's a scary place to be.

New Tools

We still mess up our races from time to time. We stumble, run off track, get ahead of our team, and even end up in an exhausted heap of discouragement again. The difference now is that we have the tools to diagnose what went wrong, get fixed up, and set off on our way again. Instead of panicking, we head back to *Reset* garage for some repair and recalibration. Having been through it before, however, we can move through much quicker this time and get back on track and on pace again.

New Service Plan

When I work out, I may not feel thirsty, but I take regular drinks of water because I know that if I don't, I will have a severe headache due to dehydration later in the evening. That's why, even without waiting for a crisis, I regularly and voluntarily return to *Reset* garage for a tune-up, minor repairs, and replenishment. I encourage you to do the same. Every month initially, then every quarter, spend some time in each repair bay, just checking that all is well and making any necessary adjustments, fine-tuning your pace and rhythm so that you can run better, wiser, and safer. As Roland Barnes says, "It's hard to derail a slow-moving train."[2]

New Spectacles

The future looks clearer and brighter because we have new spectacles with a new *focus* and a new *filter*. Instead of simply running furiously in all directions, by focusing now on our specific life purposes, we have a clear sense of why and where we are running. We frequently return to these purposes to ensure we are still on track and to encourage ourselves with our progress.

But our new spectacles also come with a unique filter that enables us to read, understand, and use research that God has allowed scientists and others to uncover. Throughout this book, we have drawn much truth directly from the Word of God, but we have also drawn on knowledge from non-Christian books.

Does this undermine or sideline God's Word?

No, because the sufficiency of Scripture means we don't

---

2. Cited in ibid.

need any more special revelation, not that we should shun every nonbiblical source of knowledge. But we use our biblical knowledge to filter nonbiblical knowledge. It was John Calvin who first used the illustration of spectacles to explain this.[3] He said that the Bible is not only what we read, but what we read with. We read all knowledge through the lens of the Bible because it is sufficient to keep us from falling into error as we read the truth God has placed in this world.

New Watchfulness

Through an encounter with our fragility, we've been reminded of our own mortality, of how short life is. We are much more conscious of the passage of time and the need to redeem it in the wisest ways possible. We relegate everything nonessential and focus only on the essentials, knowing that at the end of our time or the end of all time, we will give an account to God for our time spent here below.

New Patience

The secret to overnight success is that there is no secret. As *Fastcompany* pointed out,[4] overnight success is extremely rare. For example, Angry Birds, the best-selling game app, was software maker Rovio's fifty-second attempt at a successful program in eight almost-bankrupt years. James Dyson failed with 5,126 prototypes before perfecting his revolutionary vacuum cleaner. Norman Larsen's WD-40 lubricant got its name because his first thirty-nine experiments failed. WD-40

3. John Calvin, *Institutes of the Christian Religion*, ed. John T. McNeill, trans. Ford Lewis Battles, Library of Christian Classics, vols. 20–21 (Philadelphia: Westminster, 1960), 1.6.1.

4. Josh Linkner, "The Dirty Little Secret of Overnight Successes," *Fastcompany*, April 3, 2012, http://www.fastcompany.com/1826976/dirty-little-secret-overnight-successes.

literally stands for "Water Displacement—40th Attempt." These innovators succeeded because they humbly embraced their mistakes, used them as opportunities to learn, and continued to persevere as each shot got them nearer the bull's-eye.

Many of us burned out, crashed, or ended up depressed because we were driving too fast, or we gave up, discouraged by our failures and disappointments. But *Reset* garage has taught us to run more patiently and perseveringly, even through many difficulties.

New Balance[5]

Try to imagine your life on a chart with a number of columns: family, work, church, decisions, finances, media, people, technology, traffic, information, choices, and so on. Your energy capacity is divided between each column at the start of each day, and each moment of the day drains the energy from one column, depending on what you are doing.

Before *Reset* garage, some of these columns, maybe most of them, had fallen below the baseline into the red. Almost every day, you used up your allocated energy and more, especially in certain columns. Post-*Reset* garage, there is much greater balance, the energy is allocated more appropriately, and, at the end of most days, each column is still above the line, still in the black.

New Habits

Although many of these new actions felt difficult and awkward at first, by repetition they have become habits, almost

---

5. See Richard Swenson, *Margin: Restoring Emotional, Physical, Financial, and Time Reserves to Overloaded Lives* (Colorado Springs: NavPress, 2004), Kindle edition, loc. 186.

automatic. Science has discovered that repetition of acts and words eventually creates new neural pathways and connections that become easier and easier for the brain to follow. Although some of these new connections can be made within a couple of weeks, even the most difficult changes can be accomplished within two months. And if that's possible without the Holy Spirit, how much more with him?

New Spectators

Prior to *Reset*, we were far too engaged in man pleasing, a common symptom of a burned-out life. We were running to be noticed and praised by others. We were perhaps overmotivated by numbers: Facebook friends and likes, Twitter hearts and retweets, blog comments, and so on. For pastors, the numbers involved church members, baptisms, church plants, books, conference invitations, people evangelized, and so on. We'd lost sight of the only spectator who really matters—the Lord. Now we run to please him, looking to Jesus, the author and finisher of our faith (Heb. 12:2).

New Humility

A school principal told me that when he returned to school for the first time after a couple of weeks' absence due to burnout, "as I walked into the hallway, a crying child accompanied by a few others walked in and walked right past me to the acting principal. Hit me pretty hard. No one indeed is indispensable. Maybe the janitor but not the principal. I knew it, yet I didn't."

Elizabeth Moyer describes the humbling relief of learning to substitute dependence for independence:

The most stressful seasons in my life climax in a moment when I realize I can't do it all. I am reminded of my human finiteness and fallibility. Instead of losing my breath in anxiety, I should be able to breathe a deep sigh of relief. I can't do it all, but I don't have to. I am not enough, but Christ is. If the Creator of the universe loves me enough to die and take away all my ugly sin, then he cares about the pressures of life that bear down on me daily.[6]

When we look back at the floor of *Reset* garage, we can see a pile of rusty and broken bits and pieces that we've happily left behind: independence, self-sufficiency, self-confidence, indispensability, and invincibility.

New Grace

Reset garage shreds our sweaty performance metrics and opens our hearts to receive more of God's refreshing grace. In a blog post titled "Freedom from the Performance Treadmill," Pastor Paul Tautges testified to how Jerry Bridges's book *Transforming Grace* delivered him from the frustration and depression of thinking of himself "only as a constant failure who could never measure up to my perfectionist expectations and, therefore, did not feel fully accepted by God. . . . I had shifted the basis of my acceptance with God from his grace alone to his grace *plus* my daily performance for him." The particular section of Bridges's book that pulled the plug on this treadmill was this paragraph:

> Living by grace instead of by works means you are free from the performance treadmill. It means God has already

---

6. Elizabeth Moyer, "What Is a Biblical Response to Stress?" Institute for Faith, Work & Economics, March 16, 2016, https://tifwe.org/a-biblical-response-to-stress/.

given you an "A" when you deserved an "F." He has already given you a full day's pay even though you may have worked for only one hour. It means you don't have to perform certain spiritual disciplines to earn God's approval. Jesus Christ has already done that for you. You are loved and accepted by God through the merit of Jesus, and you are blessed by God through the merit of Jesus. Nothing you ever do will cause him to love you any more or any less. He loves you strictly by his grace given to you through Jesus.[7]

When we live a grace-based life, we not only *receive* more grace, we *give* more grace. Aware of our weaknesses and frailties, we extend more grace to others who are failing and falling. One father explained to me how "my parenting changed after I went through burnout. I suddenly realized I was asking my children to do things I couldn't do myself. I sympathized more with their struggles. There was much more talk about grace in our home. I am so thankful."

New Fruitfulness

In May 1985, Apple's mountain of unsold inventory was growing along with its debts. Sales were declining and losses were looming. Apple co-founder Steve Jobs was "relieved of operating responsibilities," and a few months later he resigned from the chairman's post to start a new computer company called NeXT.

What came next for Jobs was unexpected—twelve years

7. Jerry Bridges, *Transforming Grace: Living Confidently in God's Unfailing Love* (Colorado Springs: NavPress, 1991), 73. Cited in Paul Tautges, "Freedom from the Performance Treadmill," *Counseling One Another*, March 19, 2016, http://counselingone another.com/2016/03/19/freedom-from-the-performance-treadmill-2/.

in the corporate wilderness. Twelve years of painful, dispiriting, humiliating, stressful failure. His vision was to build a high-powered personal mainframe computer for students. He was advised to keep the price under $2,000, but ended up going to market with an underpowered computer carrying a $6,500 price tag—for students! The printer alone was another $2,000. When students didn't bite, Jobs started trying to sell to businesses, but fared little better.

Jobs was invited to return to Apple in 1997, and what a return it was! Apple's business model was rotten and fermenting. Fruitful it was not. But Jobs's return turned Apple around, and the rest, as they say, is history (and billions of dollars).

What changed? All who knew Jobs agree that the wilderness years transformed him.

Randall Stross, professor of business at San Jose State University, commented: "The Steve Jobs who returned to Apple was a much more capable leader—precisely because he had been badly banged up. He had spent twelve tumultuous, painful years failing to find a way to make the new company profitable."[8] Tim Bajarin, president of Creative Strategies, said: "I am convinced that he would not have been as successful after his return at Apple if he hadn't gone through his wilderness experience at NeXT."[9]

The idea of a life-transforming wilderness experience is nothing new to the Christian, of course. Moses, David, and even our Lord himself went to Wilderness University. Nobody wants to study there, but God sometimes sees fit to send us

8. Randall Stross, "What Steve Jobs Learned in the Wilderness," *The New York Times*, October 2, 2010, http://www.nytimes.com/2010/10/03/business/03digi.html.
9. Cited in ibid.

there. I've been enrolled there a couple of times, learning again and again that God often bruises and breaks us to prepare us for future usefulness and fruitfulness.

If you picked up this book, there's a good chance that God has enrolled you in WU, though you may be reluctant to attend classes. Sometimes I find men who are afraid to admit they need a reset. They are scared of what they will find out about themselves and apprehensive about what changes will be required in their lives. When I talk to them about the adjustments they need to make, they often resist. When I tell them they have to go 20 percent slower, sleep 20 percent more, or reduce ministry service by 20 percent, what they hear is: "Life is over, I'm a has-been, I'm just a lazy and unfruitful servant." For most of them, however, doing 20 percent less simply takes them down to about 120 percent of what most normal people do with their lives! Less does not mean nothing. *Some* change does not mean *total* change.

And, strangely, the vast majority of them eventually tell me that life on this side of *Reset* garage has turned out to be even more profitable and abundant. They are doing less but accomplishing more. They have reduced their work a little, but have seen God work much more. They have been to Wilderness University, but have graduated with baskets full of fruit.

New Christ

Many men who have experienced a breakdown or burnout have told me about how much more they have learned about Christ, especially his humanity. This gain was illustrated perfectly in Brad Andrews's article "Limitless Grace for Limited Leaders," in which he wrote:

We can only rest in our limitedness when we see that Jesus limited himself by leaving the culture of the Trinity and entering the culture of man for our sake. His act of incarnation and redemption settles our need for significance on this side of eternity. Healthy leaders accept their limits because when we look to Jesus, we see the ultimate limitation—God becoming flesh and blood to bring us spiritual rescue. And as we rest in this truth, we can let the unlimited One and his limitless grace give us courage to be the limited leader that we are and in the end, flourish for the good of our churches and the gospel.[10]

New Hope

We have experienced God's resurrection power in our lives, which gives us tremendous confidence to face the future and even face up to old problems and challenges that previously crushed us. We no longer depend on our own limited resources of reason and persuasion, but trust in God's resurrection power to change people and places.

That brings us to our ultimate hope of the ultimate resurrection.

New Horizon

Prior to *Reset* garage, many of us hardly ever looked up. We just saw the next to-do item, put our heads down, and plowed through it. We saw the next meeting, the next report, the next business trip, the next sermon, the next book, the next counseling session, and so on. But we never saw the next *life*.

Reset garage has resurrected resurrection hope. The mini-

---

10. Brad Andrews, "Limitless Grace for Limited Leaders," *For the Church*, February 29, 2016, http://ftc.co/resource-library/1/1933.

resurrection we've experienced here has given us a taste of the ultimate resurrection ahead, when every ache and pain, every cry and depression, every loss and weakness will be no more. It has also slowed our pace enough to allow us the time and space to look ahead and enjoy that view, to anticipate that final destination, where we will experience that "the sufferings of this present time are not worthy to be compared with the glory which shall be revealed" (Rom. 8:18). A grace-paced life transports us into a grace- and glory-filled eternity.

Let's run in such a way that we may be able to say: "I have fought the good fight, I have finished the race, I have kept the faith. Finally, there is laid up for me the crown of righteousness, which the Lord, the righteous Judge, will give to me on that Day, and not to me only but also to all who have loved His appearing" (2 Tim. 4:7–8). Let's run so that we may obtain the prize, the prize of all things new.

Acknowledgments

This book would not have been possible without the Christian men who have entrusted themselves and their stories to me over the years, especially those who did so for the purposes of this book. Many godly men have poured out their hearts to me from places of brokenness, weakness, and vulnerability, and have worked together with me in gradually learning how to live grace-paced lives in a burnout culture. I have learned much from them and with them, and wish to take this opportunity to salute their faith, courage, and transparency. Brothers, I've changed your names in this book to protect your privacy, but I hope you can be encouraged that God is using your painful experiences to heal and help others who have crashed and burned.

I'm deeply grateful to Justin Taylor, executive vice president of book publishing at Crossway, for initiating this book and inviting me to write it, and for the ideas that he suggested might form the basis of it. Already committed to a major long-term research project, I was not looking for another writing assignment at the time. But Justin's enthusiasm lit my fire and energized me with the prospect that a book such as this could bless many Christian men, and perhaps ministry leaders especially. As someone who has learned much from Justin's blog and books, and from watching him humbly steward his influence and leadership for the cause of Christ, I count it a privilege to labor with him in the gospel in this way. Special thanks also to Justin's support team at Crossway, not least the premier editing skills of Greg Bailey.

I'm thankful to the board and faculty members of Puritan Reformed Theological Seminary, who constantly encourage me to write for the wider church and give me every opportunity to do so.

And to my beloved Shona, thank you for running the race of life with me for twenty-five years. Thank you for helping me through *Reset* garage, more than once, and for patiently teaching me how to live a grace-paced life in a burnout culture.

General Index

abuse, 147
acceptance, 120
accountability, 83, 132, 136, 163, 180
accuracy, 44
adaptation, 120
addiction, 50, 148
administration, 154
adultery, 106–7, 161, 167
advice, 80
aging, 47, 105, 147
agreed roles, 163
Åkerstedt, Torbjörn, 58
alarm clock, 94
alcohol, 26, 60, 116–17
"always-on" culture, 133
American Psychological Association, 15
Andressen, Mark, 60
Andrews, Brad, 189–90
anger, 90, 129
Angry Birds, 183
annual bump, 102–3
anthropology, 146
antidepressants, 79, 86, 99, 146–50
antioxidants, 143
anxiety, 27, 29, 34, 48, 58, 65, 66, 89, 141, 158
apathy, 29

Armstrong, Aaron, 31
arrogance, 53–54
audit, 135
authenticity, 169
avoidance, 29
awe, 155

back pain, 25
backsliding, 34, 46, 51
bad examples, 47
Bajarin, Tim, 188
balance, 116–17, 151, 165, 184
Barnes, Roland, 182
Batzig, Nick, 177
bedtime, 164
behavior, 58, 60
bereavement, 45, 105, 152
betrayal, 172
Bezos, Jeff, 59–60
bitterness, 29
black ice, 21
blessing, 48
blood, of Christ, 76–77, 90
blood clots, 19–20, 22, 37–38
blood-sugar levels, 51, 144
boasting, 114
body, 41, 55, 73–77, 148
Bolt, Usain, 57
books, 159–60
boredom, 30

Boyd, Brady, 10, 153–54
brain injury, 147
brainwashing, 169
breakdown, 23–25, 118
breakfast, 143
breakthroughs, 118
breathing, 97
breathlessness, 25
Bridges, Jerry, 186–87
Briggs, J. R., 24, 100, 118
brokenness, 11
Brooks, David, 124–26, 161
Bullock, Sandra, 161
burnout, 11, 15, 23–25, 34, 185
Bush, George W., 71
busyness, 24, 50, 119, 151, 168
Butler, Samuel, 103

caffeine, 64
calendar, 132–33
calling, 109, 127
calm, 88
Calvinism, 68
Calvin, John, 183
cancer, 56, 77, 171
caregiving, 45
Carey, William, 83–84
caricatures, 150
Carson, Don, 60–61
Casey, George, 71–72
causes, 33
celebration, 155
celebrities, 120–21, 167
Challenger space shuttle, 59
change, 47, 53, 120, 179, 189
chaos, 133
character, 111–12, 160
chest pains, 25
childhood abuse, 147
children, 28, 164–67
Christensen, Clayton, 124–25
Christian conferences, 23, 152
Christian service, 130–31

church, 30, 105, 107
clarity, 131, 166
Clinton, Bill, 60
coffee, 26
Collins, Jim, 136–37
commercials, 105
commitments, 123
communication, 163
communion, 95
community, 170
comparison, 49–50
compassion, 38
computer games, 64
concentration, 26
conferences, 23, 152
confession, 31
conflict, 28, 46, 151
conscience, 51, 176–77
contentment, 64–65, 177–78
counseling, 11, 60, 66–67, 151
Covenant Eyes, 163
creativity, 102
creatures, 38–43, 55
criticism, 114, 151, 166
cross-country, 9–10
culture, 11
curfew, 64
cynicism, 27

Dahl, Roald, 82
daily bumps, 91–98
daily reminders, 160
damage assessment, 37
dance, 155
danger, 32
David, 188
day off, 40, 99–101, 179
deadlines, 123
death, 43
"deathstyle," 101
debt, 49
decisions, 29
decisiveness, 50

defensiveness, 179
"definite do," 134
"delay do," 134
dementia, 78, 98
dependence, 185–86
depression
    and food, 145
    and exercise, 79
    and genetics, 45
    and insomnia, 58
    medication for, 141, 146–50
    in millennials, 15
    in pastors, 11, 99
    and reading, 97
    and relationships, 28
    and resurrection, 34
    and routine, 133
    and sovereignty of God, 48
"desire to do," 134
destination, 35
devotions, 30, 109, 159
diabetes, 77, 144
diet, 22, 50–51, 142–46
differences, 47
digital media, 91–96
diligence, 50
direction, 35
disappointment, 105, 172
discipline, 63, 100
discouragement, 83, 181
disorganization, 50
distraction, 26
divorce, 152
doctrines of grace, 12
"don't do," 134
"don't waste your life" message,
    10
doubt, 41
drainers, 151
Drucker, Peter, 139
Duke University, 172
duties, 127
Dyson, James, 183

Edlund, Matthew, 62, 63
elders, 167–68
email, 30, 138, 152, 159
embarrassment, 89
emotion, 51, 58
emotional disorder, 23
emotional health, 141
emotional numbness, 27
emotional warning lights, 27
emptiness, 50
encouragement, 85, 166, 175
energizers, 150–56
energy, 108, 178, 184
energy management, 151
enjoyment, 50
entrepreneurs, 59–60
essentialism, 137
ethics, 106
evil, 46
evolutionists, 39–40
exercise, 11, 22, 26, 40, 64, 73,
    78–83, 153
exhaustion, 25, 38
expectation, 89
extroverts, 132, 152
Exxon Valdez oil spill, 59

Facebook, 46–47, 64, 92, 93, 114,
    115, 185
failure, 51, 105, 107, 108,
    117–20, 137
faith, 65
fall, 43, 146–47
false guilt, 176–77
falsehood, 114–16
family cooperation, 64
family devotions, 109
family life, 129
family mealtime, 163
fasting, 64, 94–95
fatherhood, 91, 165
fear, 151, 158
feasts, 155

Federer, Roger, 56–57
feelings, 145
fellowship, 22, 30, 31, 162
festivals, 155
fillers, 151
filter, 182
finances, 59–60, 135
fish, 145
fishing, 43, 151
Flavel, John, 160
focus, 182
food, 22, 50–51, 142–46
forgetfulness, 26
forgiveness, 13, 118
fragility, 183
frailty, 187
friendship, 22, 102, 155, 168–73
fruitfulness, 187–89
fuel consumption, 151
functionality, 168–69
futility, 84
future, 120–21

gain, 45–46, 134
gaps, 113–14
Gates, Bill, 78
genes, 45
glory, of God, 77, 119
goals, 130–31
God
    as Creator, 39
    fatherhood of, 91, 165, 179
    glory of, 77, 119
    knowledge of, 95
    nature of, 170
    promises of, 62
    relationship with, 158–60
    sovereignty of, 14, 54–55, 100,
        155
gold, 35
goodness, 157–58
gospel, 23, 165, 179

grace
    encouragement of, 175
    five deficits of, 12–15
    giving of, 186–87
    and peace, 88
    rhythms of, 103
    and truth, 41
    and work, 68
grace moderation, 17
grace motivation, 17
gratitude, 119, 151
greed, 48–49, 89, 90
Greene, Mark, 169
Groothuis, Douglas, 95
Grothaus, Michael, 97
growth, 129, 172–73
guarded time, 158
guilt, 29, 31, 89, 90, 154, 176–77,
    179

habits, 81–82, 184–85
hammers, 51–52
happiness, 45, 86, 87, 124, 153,
    155, 161–62
Harris, Dan, 87–88, 96
Harris, Josh, 32–33
Hart, Archibald, 66
Harvard Business School, 124
hate, 89
headaches, 25
healing, 146
health, 21, 25, 56, 106
heart disease, 56, 77, 171
heaven, 70
Heintzman, Paul, 154–55
high blood pressure, 56
Hill, Grant, 57
hippocampus, 78–79, 96
hobby, 84, 152
Hoehn, Charlie, 46, 58
Hollywood, 105, 109, 169
Holmes, Jonathan, 170
Holy Spirit, 76, 185
honesty, 49, 172, 177

hope, 34, 190
hopelessness, 27
horizon, 190–91
hospitality, 155
Huffington, Arianna, 53
humanity, 13, 38, 43, 44, 146–47, 180
humiliation, 80
humility, 67–68, 165, 185–86
Hybels, Bill, 38
hypercriticism, 27
hypertension, 99

identity, 42, 50, 105–21
idleness, 103
idolatry, 48, 55
ignorance, 150
illness, 45, 100, 107, 115–16, 152
ill will, 89
image of God, 126, 130, 170
imperfections, 13
indecision, 29
independence, 185–86
indiscipline, 50
indispensability, 186
infection, 56
infertility, 56
injustice, 46
inner orchestra, 88–90
innovators, 183–84
insomnia, 26, 58, 65
instructions, 39
intensity, 68
interactive media, 92
Internet, 29, 163
introverts, 111, 152
invincibility, 186
Iraq War, 71
irritation, 28

James, Lebron, 57
jealousy, 42

Jesus Christ, 189–90
  blood of, 76–77, 90
  body of, 75
  friendship with, 171
  imitation of, 121
  life of, 127
  merit of, 187
  resurrection of, 34
  as Savior, 70
Job, 34–35
job loss, 153
Jobs, Steve, 78, 117, 187–88
Jones, Mark, 160
journey, 157
joy, 23, 27, 29, 34, 178–79
junk food, 26, 50–51, 145

kakorrhaphiophobia, 117
Keane, Jack, 71–72
Kinman, Gail, 133
knowledge, 62–63, 95, 183
Kraft, Dave, 160
Kramer, Steven, 155
Kreider, Tim, 50, 103

language, 29
Larsen, Norman, 183
laughter, 27, 151, 164
laziness, 51
leaders, 16–17
legalism, 12–13
leisure, 154–55
lethargy, 25
life plan, 127
life situation, 44
lifestyle, 44, 48–51, 176
LifeWay, 167
limitations, 13, 42–43, 55, 67, 173
Lloyd-Jones, David Martyn, 102
loss, 45
Loughborough University, 64
love, 118
Lovelace, Richard, 112–13

Luebeck University, 57
lust, 129

MacArthur, Douglas, 72
magic formula, 139–40
malice, 89
manual work, 83–86
margin, 135
marriage, 27, 45, 106–7, 152, 161–64, 166, 180
Marshall, George, 72
Martin, Al, 40
masculinity, 169
Massachusetts Institute of Technology, 94
McClatchy, Steve, 134–35
McGinnis, Alan, 170
McKeown, Greg, 28, 131, 137–38
mealtime, 163
means of grace, 22
media diet, 51
media fast, 64, 94–95
medications, 146–50
meditation, 46, 87
megastress, 132
memories, 102
memory, 144
men, 15–16
mental breakdown, 23
mental disorders, 146
mental health, 141
mental illness, 167–68
mental warning lights, 26–27
middle age, 15
millennial generation, 15
mind, 142–44
mindfulness, 87
minimalism, 137
ministry, 61–62, 118, 137, 167
ministry calling, 109
ministry leaders, 16–17
mirror image, 109–10
misunderstanding, 150, 172

moderation, 12–13, 17
money, 15, 161
mood, 58, 69, 79, 142, 144–46
morality, 60
moral lapse, 23
moral warning lights, 29–30
mortality, 78, 183
Moses, 188
motivation, 12, 17, 29, 80–81
Moule, Handley, 113
movies, 29, 64, 73
moving, 46
Moyer, Elizabeth, 185–86
Muller, Wayne, 100
multiplying, 13–14
Murray, Shona, 16, 19, 44, 80, 116, 132, 162–64
music, 96
muting notifications, 93

Nadal, Rafael, 57
napping, 69
NASA, 69
National Highway Traffic Safety Administration, 59
navel gazing, 24
negativity, 114, 152
new horizon, 190–91
newness, 175
Neyfakh, Leon, 101
"no," 137–39
"not goodness," 157–58
notifications, 93
numbness, 27
nutrition, 11

obesity, 77, 99
objectivity, 44
obligation, 22, 77
obsession, 148
organization, 50
overcommitment, 151
overdrinking, 30

overeating, 30
overestimating, 42
overpromising, 131–32
overscheduled, 38
overspending, 30
overwhelmed, 38
overwork, 24, 28, 75
Owen, John, 160
Oxford University, 125

pace, 9–11, 24, 176, 191
Pace, Peter, 71
palpitations, 25
parental pressure, 105
parenting, 165
Pascal, Blaise, 95
passive media, 92
passivity, 29
pastime, 84
pastoral warning lights, 30–31
pastors, 11, 16–17, 98–99, 129,
    167–68
patience, 129, 166, 183–84
patterns, 23–24
Paul
    on boasting, 114
    on the body, 74–77
    on contentment, 177–78
    on falsehood, 116
    on identity, 112
    as tentmaker, 85
peace, 22, 88
Pelagianism, 68
people pleasing, 49, 132
perfectionism, 12–13, 49, 108,
    186
personal devotions, 30
pessimism, 27, 114
physical exercise, 11, 73, 78–83,
    153
physical projects, 85
physical warning lights, 25–26
piano, 152

Picasso, Pablo, 93
pill pushing, 141
Piper, John, 61–62
plan, 131–36
play, 82
popularity, 160
pornography, 29, 48
"post-traumatic moving syn-
    drome," 46
practicality, 33
prayer, 151, 159
Prayerful Life (PL), 140
preaching, 151, 153
prejudice, 150
"prevent-pain tasks," 135
price, 76–77
pride, 49, 105, 169
priorities, 111–12, 126, 134–35,
    170
privacy, 21
procrastination, 29, 50
productivity, 22, 24, 69, 78, 84,
    108
professionalism, 160
projects, 85
promises, of God, 62
providence, 127
prune, 136–39
Puritan Reformed Theological
    Seminary, 138
Puritans, 67, 155
purity, 129
purpose, 128–31

quarterly bump, 101–2
quietness, 22, 88, 95

"radical" message, 10
reading, 97–98, 151, 159–60
reality check, 25–35
recalibration, 181
receiving, 14–15
receptivity, 155

recovery, 146
re-creation, 43, 73
recreation, 73
Redeemer NYC, 107
reflection, 22
regret, 120, 131, 164, 165
regular study, 163
Reinke, Tony, 159
rejection, 169, 172
relational breakdown, 23
relational warning lights, 27–28
relationships
    with children, 164–67
    and depression, 28
    with friends, 168–73
    with God, 158–60
    and napping, 69
    with pastors, 167–68
    and stress, 15
    with wives, 161–62
relaxation, 22, 96
release, 14
repair, 33, 37, 181
repentance, 41–42
repetition, 185
replenishment, 154
resentment, 89
reset, 23, 33–34, 38, 152, 178,
    180–86, 190
responsibility, 47, 128
rest, 22, 31, 55, 155
resurrection, 34, 190–91
revenge, 89
review, 136
Reynolds, Adrian, 62
rhythm, 23–24, 93, 103
roles, 163
routine, 22, 63, 81–82, 133
Rowling, J. K., 117–18
running, 191

Sabbath, 99–101, 155
safety, 169

salvation, 55, 70, 75, 112
satisfaction, 84
saying "no," 137–39
Scazzero, Peter, 101
scheduling, 131
Schwartz, Tony, 57
Schwarzkopf, Norman, 160
Scripture, 40–41, 182–83
seasonal bump, 103
selectivity, 178
self-care, 24
self-centeredness, 24
self-confidence, 119, 168, 186
self-control, 60
self-denial, 50, 100
self-image, 106, 112
selfishness, 160, 168, 171
self-sufficiency, 168, 186
sensitivity, 180–81
sermonaudio.com, 159
sermons, 30, 49, 54, 153, 159
service plan, 182
sex, 27, 45
shame, 89, 149, 179
side effects, 147–48
Sigman, Aric, 171–72
silence, 90–91
sin, 34, 43, 108–9, 116–17, 147
sitting, 77–78
skinniness, 111, 114–15
sleep
    arrogance of, 53–54
    consequences of, 55–62, 159
    of pastors, 11
    vs. productivity, 22
    as theological, 54–55, 70
    as warning light, 26
sleep apnea, 69
sloth, 75
slowing down, 32
soccer, 111, 115, 120
social media, 30, 93, 105, 110,
    159, 171

Solomon, 103
sorrow, 46
soul, 41, 55, 74
sovereignty, of God, 14, 48,
    54–55, 100, 155
special periods, 68–69
spectacles, 182–83
spectators, 185
speed bumps, 91–103
spiritual character, 111–12
spiritual fellowship, 162
spiritual growth, 129, 172–73
spirituality, 106
spiritual life, 128–29
spiritual rest, 22
spiritual state, 111
spiritual warning lights, 30
sports, 56–57, 82
Spurgeon, Charles, 61
standing up, 77–78
stealing, 105
Stetzer, Ed, 168
stillness, 22
Stockholm University, 58
stomach cramps, 25
straws, 51–52
strength, 107–8
stress, 11, 15, 25, 34, 52, 66,
    123–24
strife, 34
stroke, 56, 171
Stross, Randall, 188
study, 163
success, 53, 105, 117, 119,
    183–84
suffering, 34, 124
sufficiency, of Scripture, 182–83
sugar, 76, 143, 145
Summoned Life (SL), 125–26,
    127, 139
superficiality, 169
superspirituality, 74
Swenson, Richard, 47, 139, 155

sympathy, 33–34, 119, 150
symptoms, 32

talent multiplication, 125
Tautges, Paul, 186–87
Taylor, Justin, 16
team, 180
technology, 50
temper, 28
thankfulness, 21, 32
theology, 54–55, 70, 142, 170,
    179
time management, 125, 132–33,
    151, 166
tools, 181
total depravity, 90–91
transparency, 49, 172
travel, 157
tremors, 25
Trinity, 190
true identity, 110–21
truth, 30, 41
Turkle, Sherry, 94
TV, 64, 92, 95, 169
Twitter, 185
two-income households, 99

ulcers, 25
unbelief, 50
uncertainty, 47
undistracted mind, 158–59
United Kingdom, 99, 157
United States, 11, 59, 71, 99, 100
University of Bedfordshire, 133
University of North Carolina,
    171
usefulness, 189

vacation, 102–3, 163, 179
vanity, 89, 90
Village Church, 107
Vitello, Paul, 98–99
vocabulary, 164
vocal prayers, 159

vocation, 28–29, 109, 130
vulnerability, 75

walking, 81
War and Peace, 97
Ware, Bronnie, 131
"warning lights," 25–31
watchfulness, 183
WD-40, 183–84
weakness, 15, 24, 31, 97, 107,
    187
weekends, 29
weekly bump, 98–101
weekly routine, 81–82
weight gain, 26, 51
Well-Planned Life (WPL), 124–25,
    126, 127, 128, 139

wilderness experience, 188–89
wives, 40, 49, 161–62, 165
women, 16
wonder, 155
Woods, Tiger, 57
Woodward, Bob, 72
work, 13–14, 15, 83–86
work-life balance, 165
workout, 82
world, 40–41
worry, 123
worship, 120, 166
writing, 134, 151

yoga, 87
YouTube, 96

Scripture Index

Genesis
2:18 157
3:17–19 48

Exodus
20:9–10 99
20:13 59

Job
23:1–9 34
23:10 35

Psalms
3:5 .... 55, 65
4:8 .... 55, 65
32:3–4 41
32:3–5 51
46 95
46:10 .... 22, 88
73 46
92:12–15 74
118:5 21
119:71 21
127 68
127:1–2 55
127:2 65

Proverbs
17:22 41
23:26 22
28:13 51

Ecclesiastes
3:1 103
3:2–3 103

Matthew
5:37 137
6:25–27 65
6:25–34 91
6:26 50
11:28 70

Mark
2:27 100
4:38 70
8:36 74
14:8 91

John
3:30 90
11:35 70

Acts
17:26 49

Romans
6:11 116
8:18 191
8:28 117
12:19 90

206   *Scripture Index*

1 Corinthians
6:9–10 74
6:9–20 74
6:11 74
6:12 75
6:13–14...........75
6:15–17...........75
6:18–19...........76
6:20 ....76, 77
9:24 176
10:31.............142
14:33.............133
15:10.............112, 114

2 Corinthians
4:16 74
8:9................90

Ephesians
1 112
1:1–14 112

Philippians
4:8................51
4:11–13...........177
4:13 43

1 Thessalonians
4:14 70

2 Timothy
4:7–8..............191

Hebrews
4:9................70
12:1–2 17
12:2 185

James
5:12 137

1 John
3:1................121
3:2................121
3:3................121

Cultivate a Sustainable Pace in an Overwhelming World.

Writing to women in the midst of our busy, do-it-all culture, husband-and-wife team Shona and David Murray offer practical tips for avoiding exhaustion, depression, and anxiety by setting healthy, biblical priorities motivated by Christ's transforming grace.

For more information, visit crossway.org.